VISIONS
BEFORE
MIDNIGHT

VISIONS

BEFORE
MIDNIGHT

Television criticism from
the Observer 1972-76

Clive James

JONATHAN CAPE
THIRTY BEDFORD SQUARE LONDON

First published 1977

Text © 1972, 1973, 1974, 1975, 1976 by the Observer
Preface © 1977 by Clive James

Jonathan Cape Ltd, 30 Bedford Square
London WC1

British Library Cataloguing in Publication Data

James, Clive
Visions before midnight: television
criticism from the Observer, 1972–76.
ISBN 0–224–01386–6
1. Title 2. 'Observer'
791.45'0941   PN1992.3.G7
Television programs – Great Britain – Reviews

Printed in Great Britain by The Anchor Press Ltd
and bound by Wm Brendon & Son Ltd
both of Tiptree, Essex

To Pete Atkin

Contents

CONTENTS

Dreams out of the ivory gate, and visions before midnight.

SIR THOMAS BROWNE

Preface

This book is the incidental result of my first four years as the *Observer*'s television critic. I say 'incidental' because when I began writing the column I had only fleeting notions of preserving any of it for posterity. Before coming to the *Observer* I had been one of a quartet of writers who did the occasional stint – each of us contributing one piece per month, turn and turn about – for the *Listener*, whose then editor, Karl Miller, was gratifyingly insistent that literary journalism ought to be written from deep personal commitment and to the highest standards of cogency the writer could attain. Quite apart from the eternal debt I owe him for allowing me to review television after having failed so conspicuously to become interested in reviewing radio, I shall always be grateful that his belief in the importance of what we were all up to took the tangible form of a severe discipline when it came to editing copy – which he preferred to do with the author present, so that obscurities could be explained to him by their perpetrators. The obscurities usually turned out to be solecisms.

Having your thousand words scrutinised by Karl Miller could be an experience either hilarious or scarifying, but it was rarely anything in between. I once came into the office to find him sitting behind his desk with an umbrella up, 'to ward off my troubles'. When he was in the mood to scorn the follies of the day, his invective would have me aching with laughter, and the morning flew. But when he was in the mood to be bloody, I found it intolerable to stay in the same building, and I flew instead. If I had got him carpeted before the BBC hierarchs by attacking some politician or academic for striking attitudes on the box, Miller would defend me without even telling me about it; his Calvinistic moral strength needed no bolstering from approval. On the other hand, if he suspected me of professional dereliction, however minor, his wrath shook the walls. Since I suffer from an unduly thin skin, my days with the *Listener* were consequently numbered from the beginning, but I will always look back on them with fondness. It was Karl Miller who gave me the courage of my apparent lack of convictions – or, to put it less sententiously, who let me write a column which eschewed solemnity so thoroughly that it courted the frivolous. 'And I suppose', he would say, holding his blue pencil like a blunt hypodermic about to be thrown into my upper arm, 'you've done another *cabaret turn*.' But like Lichtenberg he appreciated the kind of joke that unveils a problem: if your gags had a serious reason for being there, they stayed in. On the other hand any platitude, no matter how gravely expressed, was ruthlessly extirpated. It meant a lot to me to be able to make him laugh, because he never laughed at anybody who was merely trying to be funny.

Unfortunately as a television critic for the *Listener* I could hope to net only about £7 a week. As the television critic for the *Observer* I would do a bit better than that, with four times as many chances per month to instruct the world. There was my family to feed, not to mention my ambition. So there could be no doubt about whether or not to take up the *Observer*'s offer when it came, even though the editor of the *Listener* – more Calvinistic than ever when it came to matters of loyalty – would undoubtedly never forgive me for betraying his trust. Under a cloud was the only way anyone ever left *him*. When I turned up on jelly legs to inform him of my decision, the news had already reached him on the tom-toms. He tried to fire me as I walked through the door, but my letter of resignation was in my pocket. I left it with his secretary and high-tailed it out of the blast area. We have never spoken since, but if this book has any virtues they owe a lot to his influence.

And so my career as a weekly television columnist began. It felt straight away, and still feels now, almost illegal to be paid for having such a good time. As happens so often when your life takes a serendipitous course, the reasons arrive after the event. In retrospect it might seem as if you thought everything out but if you remember a bit harder you can usually recollect being impelled by nothing more exalted than a vague feeling of 'why not?'. There were (there still are) plenty of wiser heads to tell me I should avoid lavishing my attention on lowly ephemera, but I couldn't see why I shouldn't, if I felt like it. It wasn't that I didn't rate my attention that high – just that I didn't rate the ephemera that low. Television was a natural part of my life. I loved watching it and I loved being on it. The second passion has since somewhat faded, but the first remains strong, and was very powerful at the time. I watched just about everything, including the junk, which was often as edifying as the quality material and sometimes more so. The screen teemed with unsummable activity. It was full of visions, legends, myths, fables. And the most fabulous characters of all were those fictional ones who thought that they were factual.

Around and beyond its drama programmes, television itself was one huge drama with a cast of millions, a feature list of thousands, and starring (in no order, not even alphabetical) hundreds upon hundreds of people whose regular prominence conferred on their every peculiarity and mannerism an almost numinous ontological definition. Nobody, not even Dickens, could invent a character like Joseph Cooper and his silent piano. Patrick Moore! Esther Rantzen *putting* the *emphasis* on *every* second *word*! Bob McKenzie and his psensational psephological machines!

And somehow the cast was never diminished, only aug-mented. Out of the Women's Lib upheaval came the BBC's token lady newsreader, Angela Rippon, for ever afterwards to be cherished as Angie Cool. Out of a nightmare by Bram Stoker came the incredible Magnus Pyke, coiling and uncoiling around the studio like one of those wire toys that walk down stairs.

On top of all the stuff on television that it was my duty to talk about – plays, documentaries, series, variety shows, news – there was all this other stuff begging to be talked about as well. Raymond Williams, the most responsible of television critics, objected to what he called the 'flow' of television: the way its different component parts allegedly became stylistically homogenised into a stream of uniform unmeaning. To me, perhaps because I was an irresponsible critic, it didn't look like that. Television, in Britain at any rate, was scarcely something you could feel superior to. It was too various.

If I thought at all about my aims, it was the variety of television – the multiplicity of ways in which it engaged your interest – that I was concerned to reflect. What I had to offer was negative capability, a capacity for submission to the medium. True, other critics before me had submitted themselves to *Coronation Street* and found it instructive. But I was the first to submit myself to Alastair Burnet and find him fascinating. No critic before me had ever regarded David Vine as a reason for switching the set *on*.

Not much of a claim to individuality perhaps, but there it is. And anyway, a lot of readers seemed to feel the same. No sooner had I reviewed the performance of the BBC sports commentators at the Munich Olympics than letters started arriving to prove that David Coleman aroused the same kind of perturbed reverence in other people as he did in me. Television columnists get bigger mail-bags than other critics for the simple reason that nearly everybody watches television and has opinions about it. Whatever kind of aesthetic event television might be, it was certainly a universal one. That, at any rate, was my defence when called upon to justify my activities – which I frequently was, and never more searchingly than by Kenneth Tynan.

The scene switches to the Garrick Club. Not long after Princess Anne's wedding the *Observer*'s editor, David Astor, threw a reception there for his journalists and critics. I remember the occasion for two main reasons. The first was sartorial. Benny Green and I, raffish dressers both, turned up in an electric blue pullover and a Hawaiian shirt respectively. Faced with the spectacle we presented, a quiet voice in the lobby said, 'Mmm. Unusual.' If the voice had belonged to a venerable member I would soon have forgotten my embarrassment. But it belonged to a cleaner. The second reason was weightier. After David Astor and I had exchanged mutually indecipherable pleasantries (his shyness taking the form of pregnant pauses and mine of hollow volubility), I found myself talking to Tynan, resplendent in a leaf-green shantung Dr No jacket and full of encouragement for my efforts. When, he asked, would I be turning my critical gaze away from television and towards its proper object, the theatre? Never, was my reply. (I wish it had been firmly expressed, but I was in some awe of Tynan and tended to produce a stammer that matched his.) Tynan was thunderstruck: surely I didn't pretend that television could equal the theatre for immediacy, the feeling of occasion, the tang of life lived? 'I still get a thrill every time the curtain goes up,' he said. 'I get a thrill every time it goes down,' I replied. Those were our exact words. If the two speeches had not been separated by five minutes of random conversation they might have counted as epigrammatic dialogue. As it was, though, our different viewpoints were clearly enough expressed. I thought very highly of Tynan's theatre criticism, especially his earlier work: *He That Plays the King* I had always regarded as a magic book. But I couldn't stand the theatre. Conversely Tynan thought little of television, but was generous enough to be interested in what I had to say about it. He said he hoped that I would be publishing a selection of my pieces when the time came.

From then on the idea was in my mind. But I never let it affect the way I wrote the column, which after four years amounted to something like a quarter of a million words. Trimming such a heap of verbiage down to publishable length has entailed leaving out a good number of would-be substantial peces along with nearly all the trivia. In some ways it is the trivia which I most regret having to sacrifice, since it was through them that I came nearest to celebrating the multifariousness of what was permanently on offer for the price of a licence fee. Here and there through the book I have left a column intact, complete with its tail-end one-liners about Harry Hawkins opening and closing doors, or what the Pakenham clan got up to that week. But on the whole I have had to accept that a book which contained all my favourite paragraphs would make no sense.

For a while I toyed with the notion of transferring what I fancied to be golden phrases from columns marked for the chop to columns I proposed to keep, but to do too much of that would have been cheating. That bit about the Osmond fans using the tops of Minis as trampolines to bounce over the riot-fences into Television Centre and run wild through the corridors covering everything with regurgitated Farex — couldn't I get that bit in somewhere? But no: out it went. And bigger things went out along with it, for different reasons. There is not much left in about Ireland or Vietnam or the Middle East — not because television seldom treated them, or because I seldom wrote about the resulting programmes, but because I seldom managed to say anything particularly illuminating. It isn't enough for criticism to prove itself concerned. I admired the Jack Gold production of *Arturo Ui* and wrote a whole column about it, but now I see that I was too eager to grind an axe about Brecht: to preserve the piece I would have to rewrite it. The same applies to a rave review of *Long Day's Journey Into Night*, produced by Michael Blakemore and starring Laurence Olivier. If I cut out the superlatives, there would be nothing left: I had been so eager to transmit my enthusiasm that I never got down to brass tacks.

But if some of the big themes are gone, others remain. I have conferred a specious neatness to the book's outer boundaries by beginning with the Olympic Games at Munich and ending with them again at Montreal, so that the ineffable BBC sports commentators are there at the finish as well as at the start. Through the period of the Olympiad bulk some grand events, real and imagined: *War and Peace*, the Royal Wedding, Nixon's fall, the General Election, Margaret Thatcher's rise, *The Glittering Prizes*, Solzhenitsyn's expulsion. Since the book can't pretend to contain the whole of its parent column, and since the column can't pretend to contain the whole of television, and since television can't pretend to contain the whole of life, there is no question of chronicling everything that has happened in the world over the last four years. Nor, however, does one forgo all claims to pertinence.

Most of the blockbuster programmes get a mention, even if only a short mention. Sometimes a short mention was all they deserved. As for current events, it all depended where you looked. In twenty minutes of being interviewed by Robin Day, General Haig told you all you needed to know about the Nixon administration, simply by the havoc he wreaked on the English language. For that matter, a cameo appearance by Pierre Salinger told you most of what you needed to know about the Kennedy era. Every viewer is an amateur television critic and can judge how well he is being told something directly. What a professional television critic ought to be able to contribute is the ability to assess what he is being told indirectly. He ought to know when a blurred message about something is really a clear message about something else. Television can never give you a programme

on, say, Israel which would be a tenth as informative as
Saul Bellow's magnificent *New Yorker* articles on the same
subject. It hasn't the time and probably it hasn't the brains:
only a copiously reflective mind wielding a scrupulous prose
style can take so profound a view. But television *will* give you
a programme like *QB VII*, which in its very mediocrity tells
you exactly what happens when a historical tragedy is
popularised. Reviewing *QB VII* seemed to me just as worth-
while a critical task as reviewing Thames Television's special
two-part programme on the Final Solution, and a consider-
ably more difficult one.

Only once in the four years did I get around to pro-
nouncing on the television critic's Function. The piece is
included here under the title 'What is a television critic?' It
includes most of the points I am able to make explicitly
about that subject. Other and more important points are,
I hope, made implicitly in all the other columns, but it is
perhaps worthwhile to say one or two additional things here,
although the risk of sounding pompous is great. One of the
chief Functions of a television critic is to stay at home and
watch the programmes on an ordinary domestic receiver,
just as his readers do. If he goes to official previews, he will
meet producers and directors, start understanding their
problems, and find himself paying the inevitable price for
free sandwiches. A critic who does not keep well clear of the
World of the Media will soon lose his sting. He might also
begin harbouring delusions about his capacity to modify
official policy. In reality, even the most trenchant critic can
hope to have very little effect at executive level. On the other
hand, even the mildest critic is likely to have more effect than
he realises at the level of programme-making, where the
creative personnel are inordinately dependent on written
evidence of intelligent appreciation. If you say that there
ought to be more programmes like such and such, you will
rarely change the mind of a senior executive who has already
decided that there ought to be fewer. But you might help

give the people who made the programme the courage to persist in their course.

The critic should never imagine that he is powerful, but it would be culpable of him not to realise that he is bound to be influential. There is no reason, however, to be crushed flat by the responsibility of the job. It is, after all, a wonderfully enjoyable one, even at its most onerous. The onerousness, incidentally, springs more from the fatigue of trying to respond intelligently than from the necessary curtailment of one's night-life. Any television critic soon gets used to being asked about how he supports the loss of all those dinner parties. Doesn't he pine for intelligent conversation? The real answers to such questions are usually too rude to give, unless the interrogator is a friend. Formal dinner parties are an overrated pastime, barely serving their nominal function of introducing people to one another, and nearly always lamentably devoid of the intelligent conversation they are supposed to promote. Most people severely overestimate their powers as conversationalists, while even the few genuinely gifted chatterers tend not to flourish when hemmed about by bad listeners. The talk on the little screen is nearly always better than the talk around a dinner table. For my own part, I hear all the good conversation I need when lunching with drunken literary acquaintances in scruffy restaurants. In London, the early afternoon is the time for wit's free play. At night, it chokes in its collar.

What I miss in the evenings is not dinner parties but the opera house. When I finally give up reporting the tube, it will probably be because the lure of the opera house has become too strong to resist. But sitting down to be bored while eating is an activity I would willingly go on forgoing. The box is so much more entertaining – a fact which even the most dedicated diners-out occasionally admit, since from time to time it becomes accepted in polite society that the long-drawn-out gustatory proceedings may be interrupted in order to watch certain programmes. It was recognised, for example, that *The Glittering Prizes* might legitimately entail a concerted rush from the dinner table to the television set, although I confess that in this one case my own inclination was to rush from the television set to the dinner table.

As I compose this introduction, the future shape of television in Britain is in some doubt. I have my own opinions about what needs to be done. Some of them are strong opinions and when my turn comes to be interviewed by Lord Annan I hope I will voice them strongly enough to make them heard. But arguing about policy is something apart from the week-to-week business of criticising what comes out of the box.

One way or another, when the high matters have been discussed and settled, television in this country will go on being an enchanted window in which everything from the squint of Hughie Green to the smile of Lord Longford will suddenly appear and demand to be interpreted. The Brothers will return. The Hawk will walk. Pundits will pronounce. Literary riches will be transmuted into dross and trash will become established as myth. 'A television critic would have to know everything,' Tynan objected, 'and who knows everything?' I was lost for an answer at the time, but have found one since. It isn't necessary to know everything – just to remember that nobody else does either.

I would like to thank David Astor for having brought me to the *Observer*; Donald Trelford for having put up with me subsequently; Richard Findlater for his supervision early on; John Lucas for his scrupulous copy-editing; and above all Terry Kilmartin, *éminence grise* of the arts pages, for his wise counsel. Finally I would like to thank my wife for her invaluable criticisms of the finished text, especially the crucial suggestion that beyond a certain point it is counterproductive to go on being bad-tempered about James Burke.

C.J.

VISIONS
BEFORE
MIDNIGHT

Auntie goes to Munich

WITH more than half of the 170 scheduled hours of television coverage already delivered safely into your living-room there can't be much doubt that the star personality of these Games – the single soul in whom elegance and endurance are fused by the flame of the Olympic spirit – is Britain's gallant little Frank Bough.

There's been controversy about this man. It's been questioned whether one commentator, however gifted, should be asked to talk for the full 26 hours, 385 minutes every day of the Games. Rumours of anabolic steroids and jaw-strengthening injections have threatened to cast a shadow over the achievement of this astonishing boy from Wood Lane who did his training on *Grandstand*. But as day follows day Bough's stature grows. By now he's within an ace of overcoming that worrying upset caused by changing his speech-pattern between telecine cues, and as he finishes each evening in a flurry of collapsing elocution many people are beginning to say that Frank Bough – the boy from Television Centre who puts the emphasis *on* his prepositions and breaks into a shout when you LEAST expect it – could push BBC commentating back up there among the medals where it belongs.

Despite, however, the never-failing entertainment value of his deathless hunger for a British victory, Bough is by no means the most accomplished footler in the BBC squad: indeed, whole minutes go by when he unfascinatingly sticks to a recognisable version of the English language, and it's only in moments of sudden stress that we start hearing about Mark Spitz going for his fourth goal meddler the Games here in Munich.

Also there in Munich is plucky David Vine – the boy who learned his enunciation from Eddie Waring on *It's A Knockout* and crewed for Michael Aspel on all those beaudy commatitions that laid the foundations for Mike's career as an encyclopedia salesman. David, it turns out, can't pronounce Shane Gould. He put in an entire day of commatition calling her Shane Gold, and after a long, weary night presumably spent having his urine analysed and tiny lights shone in his eyes he racked himself up to maximum effort and succeeded in calling her Shane Gld.

For the full effect of ill-timed patriotism, lack of content and slovenly execution which marks BBC sports commentating at its finest, we need to quit headquarters and go out on location – preferably to the swimming pool, where the same voices which at winter sports take hours to tell you hardly anything about what's going on in the snow take days to tell you absolutely nothing about what's going on in the water. Diversion here is on several levels. First, and most obvious, is the punishment handed out to the English language – which on the BBC has survived, and even profited from, all kinds of regional and colonial accents, but can't be expected to go on flourishing under the tidal assault of sheer somnolence. After these Lympic Games we should be asked to hear no more of Spitz's long, easy stryle, the brack stroke, or Gunnar Larsen of Sweding.

But your paradigm no-no commentary can't be made up of fluffs alone (although if it could, Walker and Weeks would be the lads to do it). It needs flannel in lengthy widths, and it's here that Harry and Alan come through like a whole warehouse full of pyjamas. 'Every move of his', raves the voice over the action replay of Spitz knocking off yet another record he already holds, 'is concentrated into just moving through that water.'

The best camera at the pool was the overhead longitudinal one lensed and angled to speed the action instead of slowing it – the usual stodgy effect of a long lens was eliminated, and swimming has never looked more fluent. But this camera couldn't get into action without Harry and Alan chiming in with something like 'now you can see it, power personified with this boy as he comes back down this course'. Incipient lyricism was blasted in the bud.

Heights of lunacy were scaled when a British hope called Brinkley set off on the first lap of a butterfly event. 'And there's Brinkley, quite content to let Mark Spitz set the pace.' What was actually happening, of course, was that Brinkley, like all the other competitors, was already contenting himself as best he could with being totally destroyed, but thanks to our dynamic duo of commentators it was Brinkley who looked the fool. They just didn't seem to realise how asinine it was to suggest that Brinkley would have done better at the end of the race if Spitz hadn't forced him to go so fast in the first half.

The brute fact so far has been that the swimming commentaries have added nothing to the pictures except file-card titbits about little Lodja Gdnsk of Poland being born in Pfft and just missing out on a medal at the pan-European dry-pool Games at Flart. But the voices-over on the swimming are a Principia Mathematica of condensed argument compared to the vocal gas enshrouding the visuals from the diving pool. 'Here she comes, into the back position,' says our irrepressible voice as the diver walks to the end of the board and turns around, 'and look at those toes working at the end of the board: and there she goes, round into the twist and *round* and *down* and...*in*.' Television for the blind.

It needs to be said, good and loud, that the BBC's block-buster coverage of the Munich Olympics has been a pain in the ear. The directors face daunting technical problems in selecting from the lavish camerawork the Germans have laid on: to assess their accomplishments accurately you'd need to know all the other choices that were open, so apart from noting a tendency to switch away from a Russian gymnast and hurry off to watch a British canoe caught upside down in what appears to be a rotary washing-machine ('I don't want to be a pessimist,' said our commentator, 'but I think British hopes of a medal are fading') I prefer to leave that part of the job uncriticised. But the accompanying talk has rarely reached adequacy.

As for the Games themselves, they need a cure. Dr Bannister was on the right lines when he said they needed scaling down. Getting rid of the flags would be a good first step towards getting rid of the drugs. But I, for one, don't want to get rid of the Games themselves. Without them there'd be no Olga Korbut, no Ludmilla Tourischeva, no Alan Weeks, no David Vine. Without them there'd be no enchanted moments such as Barry Davies moaning dementedly, 'No team has worked harder than the winners of this match,' after Russia beat Japan at volleyball, and then adding in a concerned mutter, 'or indeed the losers.'

3–10 September, 1972

Storm over England

A FULL score of series, new and refurbished, and one all-evening blockbuster crammed the week with vitamins. Large things first: *If Britain Had Fallen* (BBC1) ran to the length of *The Sorrow and the Pity* but couldn't match it for weight. Since the occupation of France was an historical fact, a programme on the subject was able to busy itself with what the Nazis did and what the French tried to do in return. The occupation of Britain failed to occur, leaving future script-editors the problem of dealing in hypotheses, most of them vague.

For a major documentary (his fellow-officer, Major Setback, also showed up during the evening) the programme under discussion was conspicuously short of the wherewithal —the Germans just didn't have all that many plans drawn up for dealing specifically with Britain, so that concentrating

26

on their intentions turned out to be a way of dissipating the air of menace instead of thickening it.

Part 1, 'Operation Sea Lion', covered familiar ground but came up with some unfamiliar facts and footage. Two hundred thousand British dogs were destroyed as some kind of insurance against air attack, and there was film to prove that horses wore gas-masks. Hunting parties prodded haystacks to flush paratroopers, thereby demonstrating that nobody really knew much about what paratroopers were. To rub this point home, there was some diamond-sharp footage of Ju 52s remorselessly unloading battle-hungry *Fallschirmjaeger* all over Holland. The heavy implication was that Britain would have stood no chance if the Germans had got ashore in force. Few knowledgeable people quarrel with this. The further implication, though (that the Germans knew exactly what they planned to do next), didn't ring so true.

Part 2, 'Life Under the Occupation', contained as much hard news as ever existed. Harrow, Eton and the Oxbridge colleges were to become homes away from home for the SS, apparently because of the abundance of sporting facilities. Apart from the Black List, which we already knew about, there was a White List, naming indigenous sympathisers to the Nazi ideal. For libel reasons, we couldn't be told the names on it. I'd be surprised if Carlyle and Ruskin weren't among them.

Reminiscences and reconstructions of what went on in the Channel Islands provided most of the meat in this part of the show. People who were children at the time are still angry about how their homes were looted by their neighbours the moment after they were moved out for deportation. The Germans provided many islanders with a new angle on their fellow man. Apart from malnutrition, that was about all: the local Gestapo, for example, was strictly Mickey Mouse compared with what was on offer further east.

In Part 3, 'The New Order', we were given the Big Picture, numerous experts being wheeled on to deal with questions of free will and destiny. Dr William Sargant told us about the psychological techniques the Nazis would have employed to soften up the population for whatever it was they planned to do to it. What failed to emerge was a clear projection of the global future the Nazis were supposed to be dreaming of. This ideal has been described, in theoretical works on the subject of totalitarianism, as 'universal concentration'. Closer than that it's difficult to come.

Hitler's table talk was quoted – the famous, demented passage about a Russia cleaned up for use as a German holiday camp-cum-autodrome. There is no reason to think that his plans for Britain would have been anything like this: such as they were, they were probably fully as insane, but in another way. It was amusing, in this context, to find the delectable Sir Oswald Mosley being interviewed. 'I think most people watching you now would have expected you to become Hitler's representative in this country.' 'Why?' Apparently he was all set to commit suicide instead.

Running through all three parts of the programme was the question of who would have resisted and who collaborated. The answer was hard to find. The next evening, on *Line-up* (BBC2), Lord Boothby was certain that resistance would have been concerted and unceasing. As it happened, the nation's heroism in the grip of the oppressor was never tested, reinforcing the perennial, guilty suspicion that Britain's liberties are dependent on innocence – the suspicion out of which programmes like this arise. It's a national characteristic, and a civilising one. So is a sense of the absurd. Enoch Powell was also on *Line-up* insisting that he, too, would have committed suicide. Perhaps Mosley would have lent him a gun.

It was a tense week for current affairs. *World in Action* (Granada) divested an anti-immigration agitator of his placard and flew him down to Uganda to suss out the scene from up close. The communication fallacy worked full blast in both directions. 'What do you fink abaht the Asians?' 'De onions?' 'Nah, the *Asians.*' Semantic malfunctions not-withstanding, our hero ended up admitting that fings were more complicated than he'd fought.

17 September, 1972

Overture to War and Peace

EVERY other critic in town has by now completed his preliminary estimation of *War and Peace* (BBC2) and quit the examination hall, leaving this writer alone in draughty silence. At this rate people are going to start suspecting that I haven't read the book. The smell of fear rises damply.

The Big Question stands out on the examination paper in letters of fire. Compulsively I footle with the little questions, half hoping that my sketchy answers will add up to something. It must be terrific to be a Marxist. And even better to be Nancy Banks-Smith: she just came straight out and *said* she hadn't read the book. I don't know much about Yasnaya Polyana but I know what I like – that's the line to take. Only I have read the book. Except I can't say that because people will think I've read it *specially.* Jings, look at the clock. And I haven't even finished writing about *Six Faces.* Talking about Kenneth More when everybody else is on about Anthony Hopkins. I wonder what Kenneth More would have been like as Pierre. As Pierre Bezukhov, the legless Russian pilot. Concentrate ... That new series, *The Pathfinders* (Thames), has got pilots in it, but they've all got legs. Mine have gone to sleep.

Six Faces (BBC2) has now clocked up two episodes, like *War and ...* No, wrong approach. *Six Faces* has now presented us with two of the promised six aspects of its leading character, a worried businessman played by Kenneth More. More has never been among my favourite actors, first of all because of his unshakeable conviction that the expletive Ha-ha! delivered straight to camera conveys mirth, and secondly because he has not done enough to quell the delusion, prevalent among the populace of the Home Counties, that he was responsible for the defeat of the Luftwaffe in 1940. Nevertheless, he is very good in this series, using a certain crumpled puffiness, or puffed crumpledness, to hypnotic effect: the complex pressures working even in sheer plodding ordinariness have rarely been better registered, and the series already bids fair to leave us pondering on all the weary little ways a salesman meets his death.

The Incredible Robert Baldick (BBC1) stars Robert Hardy as the Incredible, and should rate like mad: it's a kind of take-home Hammer film wrapped in silver foil. The well-heeled hero is a piece of nineteenth-century fuzz dedicated to fighting evil in its more occult manifestations. He steams about in a special train – which should add the railway nuts to the horoscope consulters and swell the ratings even further. Precociously democratic, the Incredible has a pair of polymath servants who ask, 'Doctor, what are we up against?' and when he answers, 'All in good time, all in good time,' gaze at him in wondering worship instead of crowning him with the fire-tongs.

Mrs Warren's Profession (BBC2) showed that Coral Brown is as good at Shaw as *Lady Windermere's Fan* proved she was good at Wilde. Other actresses, among whom Maggie Smith shall be nameless, should take a long look and painlessly absorb a few hints on how not to go over the top on the tube: *The Millionairess* (BBC1) would have benefited from a bit less irrepressible theatricality in the title role.

8 October, 1972

Tolstoy makes Television History

D EAD ground is the territory you can't judge the
extent of until you approach it: seen from a distance, it
is unseen. Almost uniquely amongst imagined countries,
Tolstoy's psychological landscape is without dead ground —
the entire vista of human experience is lit up with an equal,
shadowless intensity, so that separateness and clarity continue
even to the horizon.

This creative characteristic is so powerful in Tolstoy that
we go on regarding it as his most important distinguishing
mark even when his progressively doctrinaire intellect
imposes the very stereotypes and moralistic schemes which
his talent apparently came into existence to discredit. The
formal perfection and retributive plot of *Anna Karenina* don't,
we feel, represent an artistic advance on *War and Peace* —
quite the reverse. And yet we never call our reservations
disappointments, any more than we are disappointed with
Titian's last phase or the original, Great Fugue ending to
Opus 130. If a great talent pushes on beyond what we have
loved in it, it is usually because a great mind has things it
feels forced to do.

Besides, Tolstoy's gift remains so obviously the *same* gift,
from first to last, that it does our criticism for us: in *War and
Peace* Napoleon is an unsatisfactory characterisation accord-
ing to the standards set by Tolstoy himself (in Kutuzov, for
example) and even in the most inflexible of the moral
parables ('How Much Land Does a Man Need?' or — to go
the whole hog — 'Resurrection') we are obviously in the
presence of the same all-comprehending vision that brought
back its clinically objective reports from the bastions at
Sebastopol. Any aesthetic experience obliterates all other
aesthetic experiences for as long as it lasts, and with Tolstoy
it lasts for days and days, so that the reader may feel — as he

feels with Shakespeare and Dante – that his life is being remade.

The technique of the novel, or even the medium of prose, has no separate conceptual meaning in such a context: there can be no question of transposing Tolstoy from the page to the screen, since he is not on the page in the first place. He is like Michelangelo and Mozart in that the attempt to grasp him entails a sacrifice of comprehension. Universal genius is its own medium and transpositions out of it are impossible – it's one of genius's defining characteristics. That Verdi re-created Othello in music doesn't make Othello a transferable asset. It simply means that Verdi is in Shakespeare's league.

So far, the BBC's *War and Peace* has done nothing like a good enough job of being not as good as the book, and instead of driving the viewers to read Tolstoy – which is the best, I think, that a TV adaptation could hope to do – might well lull them into thinking that Tolstoy is Russia's answer to Mary Renault. Marianne Moore wanted her poems to be artificial gardens with real toads in them. This production reverses that desirable order: the sets and costumes are as real as research and technology can make them, while the people who inhabit them are of an artificiality no amount of good acting – and there is plenty of appalling acting on tap – can defeat.

Working together as fatally as Laurel and Hardy trying to climb a wall, the script and the direction do a brilliantly thorough job of boiling Tolstoy's complexity of dialogue, commentary and revealed action down to a simple narrative line which simultaneously faithfully reproduces and utterly betrays the novel's flow of events. 'Papa's arranged a little dinner for my name day,' breathes Hélène, her piercing boobs heaving in a frock closely resembling a two-car garage: 'I hope ... you'll be there.' Pierre, valiantly played by Antony Hopkins, can only goggle, bemused. Except when the occasional voice-over supplies a brief stretch of interior monologue, goggling bemused is what Pierre goes in for full time. At Hélène's party, during which her sensational norks are practically on the table among the sweetmeats, Pierre is asked to do a worried version of the bug-eyed act Sid James turns on when he is abruptly shoved up against Barbara Windsor.

Hopkins would be the ideal Pierre if the part were nearer half-way to being adequately written, but all he can do, given the material to hand, is project the necessary inner confusion without transmitting the bashful radiance which Tolstoy stunningly insists that Pierre and Hélène share: there is no such thing as *mere* passion in Tolstoy, and even while racked by doubts Pierre is supposed to experience in his contemplation of Hélène the kind of *visione amorosa* which helps drive Anna Karenina into the arms of Vronsky. What I'm saying is, he's not just hung up on a pair of knockers, right? So those tight shots of Pierre peeking sideways through his prop specs at where his companion's lungs pulsate off-screen might look like clever direction but are in fact graffiti.

The hamming contest between the marriage-mongering old Princes is a groan-inspiring trial, but in the long run not so debilitating as principal casting that has gone wrong. Given, which one doesn't give, that the characters are types, it would have been better to cast *against* type than to cast to type — at least complexity would have been hinted at, if not embodied. Alan Dobie's whole screen persona is confined by his face and voice to the band between melancholy and preoccupation, with occasional joyful leaps upward into apprehensiveness. Putting him into uniform and calling him Andrei Bolkonsky gives us one aspect of the character while instantly eliminating all the others. As for Morag Hood's Natasha — well, I am not in the business of baiting actresses for errors of casting they did not commit and can do little to overcome. Miss Hood has been excellent in other things and will be excellent again, once she has got over being told to jump up and down rapidly on the spot, lithp with her sinuses, skip on to the set like Rebecca of Sunnybrook Farm and declare with a jaw well-nigh dislocated by youthful vitality that she is Natasha Rostov. Poor mite, can she help it if she arouses throughout the country an unquenchable desire to throw a tarpaulin over her and nail down the corners?

This is not to say that a few things have not gone right. As Princess Maria, for instance, the delicate Angela Down is turning in one of her customary elegantly modulated performances, and some of the wide-open location spaces capture your imagination for the brief time before a sequence of restricted camera movements forcibly reminds you that even the most expensive television is a very cheap movie when the cathode tube is pre-empted by emulsion. Like most people, I'll go on watching, but I won't be gripped. It's no use saying that a chance has been lost. The chance was never there. The series could have been a lot better, but my point is that it would still not have made television history. Television history is made out of television, not out of Tolstoy.

22 October, 1972

Knickers

ON *Something to Say* (Thames) Sir Isaiah Berlin and Professor Stuart Hampshire played amiable badminton across a net formed by the increasingly elaborate, cat's-cradle hand-signals of Bryan Magee, who after several months of sitting between contestants lobbing abstract concepts at each other has by now developed a precise explanatory semaphore: that gesture where the stiffened left hand brushes crumbs off the knuckles of the loosely poised right, for instance, means the tendency of class-systems to crumple under the pressure of industrialism and re-form with a new set of interior stresses.

Professor Hampshire and Sir Isaiah had plainly been through all this before – presumably in Oxford, where they have a college each. But they didn't mind cantering through it again for our benefit, eschewing too many casual mentions of Treitschke or Max Weber and simply bearing down hard on the subject, which was nationalism.

Sir Isaiah's closing point was that understanding it probably wouldn't be much help in controlling it. This position, with its corollary that knowledge should be pursued for its own sake and not for its putative social efficacy, strikes me as tough and sane – or perhaps one is merely feeling particularly helpless this week, waiting for a thalidomide child to receive a letter bomb. The logic of terrorism demands a soft target.

The second programme in BBC1's series on *The Commanders* dealt with 'Bomber' Harris, who also knew something about soft targets. Like the Rommel programme, this one was lamentably tardy in getting down to bed-rock, spending most of its time being fascinated with its own film footage – some of which was new, most of which was horrifying, and all of which raised questions which should have been central to the programme's structure rather than incidental. Harris's professed aim of inflicting unacceptable material damage on German industrial cities was gone into, but the problem of how this aim could be squared with the eventual destruction of Dresden was not.

There was a throwaway line about Dresden lying behind the Germans as they faced the advancing Russians. If this was a rehash of the hoary old face-saver about Dresden being a potential centre of resistance, then it was an effrontery. Dresden was the logical culmination of the bombing policy which started at Cologne, and that policy was terror – even if Goebbels said it was. The Nazis were barbarians and had to be put down with dreadful means; in the end our cruelty was right because theirs was wrong. But this ought to be the nub of the matter, and not an *a priori* assumption. This series, naught but the distant rumble of a Second World War juggernaut e'en now powering towards our screens, bodes as I plead – ill.

Pity and terror? The Greeks had a purge for it. The Cedric Messina production of *King Oedipus* (BBC2) had a greater coherence of interpretation than most productions emanating from that source and held the eye and mind throughout, although it lost the imagination somewhere about halfway through. The setting was the modern Middle East, with the Theban power-structure sitting about in uniforms of British descent while a constantly running buzz-track of agitated shuffling, random shots, Casbah mutterings and low-flying jet planes conveyed the impression of a fluid political situation in the environs.

Laying the triple-whammy on himself, Ian Holm as Oedipus signed off with 'er, the gods curse all who disobey this charge' in the same way that a tired businessman remains yours sincerely. Alan Webb as Teiresias surged on in a wheel-chair, simultaneously recalling Dr Strangelove and the Mercury Theatre production of *King Lear* – trace any theatrical updating back far enough and you always seem to get to Orson Welles. Oedipus telegraphed his imminent disintegration with a virtuoso neurotic quiver when Jocasta, trying to put him at his ease, said that Laius was killed at the place where three roads meet. Jocasta was Sheila Allen, which is another way of saying superb.

Why, then, with all this talent going for it – including a sumptuous lighting design that covered the decor with spiced gloom – did the production have so little real sting? The answer, I think, is that there is not much point in trying to supply a binding image to a play whose author was so intent on leaving imagery out. It's difficult to think of Sophocles looking with favour on any attempt to pin his universalised theme to mere political instability. As for the discotheque scene that degenerated into a gang-bang, and Oedipus's People high-stepping through the streets – look, knickers only *sounds* like a Greek word.

A new David Mercer play called *The Bankrupt* (BBC1) continued BBC1's recently established tradition of putting on plays about bankrupts. This one had the prestige of Mercer's name, and was a tiresome demonstration of the law that he, like John Hopkins, is likely to eke out a half-imagined idea by double-crossing his own talent and piling on precisely the undergrad-type tricksiness his sense of realism exists to discredit. Joss Ackland, a useful heavy with a seldom-explored second line in sensitive nutters, played a washed-up executive whose father didn't understand him. 'Ah never could make thee out,' said dad, conveying this incomprehension: 'Thah talks gibberish, lad.'

Subject to a recurring dream in which key figures, including dad, toured the perimeter of a pentangle in which he was trapped, our hero attracted everybody's misunderstanding except Sheila Allen's, whose peculiar fate it is to look and sound twice as humanely intellectual as any script with which she is supplied – her role as George Eliot was the only part which has so far been worthy of her magnificent screen presence. Here she proffered her bosom for Mr Ackland to bury his head in, the lucky devil. She then turned up in the dream as one of his accusers, presumably signifying that her generosity had threatened him with castration. You may have noticed that the play ended with a scream. It was mine.

3 December, 1972

Liberating Miss World

THE theme (Women's Liberation) and the pace (stilted but inexorable) were set by the ever-lovely *Miss World* (BBC1) which raised its annual kit of Platonic queries, such as – is it better to be Socrates unhappy than a pig happy?

Practically without exception, the faces are null: one searches them despairingly for a flicker of the potential supposedly awaiting release, the female creativity allegedly begging to be liberated. No soap. Just a pack of fair to middling, not unpleasing, impenetrably dopey broads.

They're the ruck which Michael Aspel exists to electrify, and although it's true that they find him wonderful because they've been told to, it's by no means true that terminating this cultural programming would result in spontaneous choices being substituted for the mechanical ones. What you would get would be the acrid fizz of overloaded circuits, whereupon the ladies would start walking into walls, sitting down in mid-air or explaining their hobbies to a pillar-box.

So far Women's Lib has had great difficulty in coping with the idea that the activities of the lumpenproletariat might simply have to be respected for themselves. One of the leading characteristics of the not-quite-bright is their disastrous over-estimation of the role of intellect in political reality. This stricture applies full force to Women's Lib, which seems intent on supposing that unintelligent behaviour is an aberration, and that naught but a male chauvinist conspiracy stops Miss Australia realising the desirability of being Germaine Greer.

The Women's Libbers shouldn't get too impressed by the undoubted truth that Germaine Greer can understand Rosa Luxemburg and Miss Australia can barely understand Michael Aspel: it's not a crime, it's just life – and by no means the worst of life, either. I used to see Miss Australia every day on the beaches around Sydney, with zinc cream on her nose. She was all right. Nothing special. Her name always turned out to be something like Gaylene Gunth. While waiting for Michael Aspel to come into her life, she'd sit around for hours on a beach-towel, pining that she had only 10 fingernails to paint. No repressive culture ever made her. She made the culture. She was as free as the ozone, as liberated as the space between the stars.

On *Talk-In* (BBC1) Robin Day chaired a discussion of *Miss World* between a handful of Women's Libbers and the massed forces of darkness. Far from being the natural output of a male chauvinist pig, Day's arrogance goes beyond sex and indeed the bounds of credibility, to the point where you expected a flying wedge of ravening Maenads to spring from the audience and rip him to bits.

Goaded by Day's raucous complacency, however, genuine conflict was not slow to emerge, and we were soon regaled with the spectacle of the assembled rhetoricians listening nonplussed to Sally Oppenheim, M.P., who is actually engaged in trying to change a few things for the better now, instead of waiting for the revolution to transmute everything into perfection. Her tough arguments embodied the difference between reality and rhetoric.

But Seriously – It's Sheila Hancock (BBC2) featured Germaine Greer being funny, which is something I'm always keen to watch. Some years ago I happened to be present when she pioneered the technique of singing 'Land of Hope and Glory' with the lips out of synch with the words – a revelation. Unfortunately there is also a tendency for the vocal chords to get out of phase with the brain, so that on this programme we heard her animadverting on the sexual prowess of her husband. The appropriate reaction to this would have been a brisk lecture on fair play, but the awed Miss Hancock was too busy being overwhelmed by her guest's intellectual stature to blow the whistle.

Granada's *The Web* was written by Alun Owen with the flawless symmetry we normally attribute to a billiard ball. Jenny Twigge's boyfriend was Michael Kitchen, but her mum was Ann Firbank, and when the boy saw the woman he forgot the girl. 'I'm what I've always wanted to be,' purred *la* Firbank, flashing him an azure armpit, 'severe and free, austere and abandoned.' She didn't read *that* in Eva Figes. 'I'm a spider called Agnes, and you don't mind my sticky web. Do you, Barry?' 'Sticky?' quavered our lad, but her flickering tongue was in his ear and there was no reply. An appalling effort.

World in Action (Granada) did a special on the Angry Brigade. Far back in the mind you could hear a giant door thumping hollowly on an era's end as the earnest Anna Mendelson informed the world that justifying your actions was a middle-class notion and that you had to do something before finding out if it was right or wrong. Make way for the Apocalypse, ladies and gents.

On *Midweek* (BBC1) there was more of the same, with Tom Mangold's report on Black September, in which it was revealed that one of the stated principles of this outfit's chief ideologues is to steer clear of the politicos and try to knock off the artists. On *Man Alive* (BBC2) Harold Williamson interviewed a man who had crippled his own baby boy. As yet unsupplied with an ideology, this character was obliged to admit that he just bashed the kid because he didn't like him. But enough. In the whispered words of Otto Preminger, delivering a repressively tolerant kiss to Joan Bakewell's hand at the N.F.T., 'I tink we should finish now.'

10 December, 1972

A living legend

THE New Year came in on great plumed and crested waves of kitsch and camp. Punch the buttons as you might, you were drowning in the perfumed effluent of rotten old Showbiz at its most outrageous. Things took place on the David Frost special (*At Last the 1973 Show*, LWT) which must remain forever nameless, but principally involved Ethel Merman giving forth with an overwhelming vibrato which could be silenced only by commercials, the enthralled Frost apparently being keen to have it continue.

How can people *be* like this, you wondered moaning, and for an answer were clobbered with the rerun of *A Star is Born* (BBC1), a titanically lousy movie whose degrading fragrance intensifies with the years and which enshrines yet another soubrette who never knew how to give less than her All.

But *de mortuis*, and anyway there was another stellar presence on the loose, and very much in command. She was the legendary, indestructible *Dietrich* (BBC2), appearing for the first time in her very own TV special, entirely shot at Bernard Delfont's gizmo-laden new theatre in which everything revolves around everything else. As we shall presently see, this ritzy culture-barn's meandering appointments must include a hot-house the size of the one at Kew, but for the moment let's rest content with conceding that at first blush it didn't look a bad test-track for an indestructible legend.

While a Burt Bacharach arrangement of 'Falling In Love Again' (complete with sour mutes on the trumpets) sounded longingly from the pit, the house lights went down and the discs of two limes randomly searched the fore-stage. The possibility that Emil Jannings might be about to appear was cancelled by a quick glance at *Radio Times*: no, Marlene it had to be. Difficult, in that case, to imagine why the lime-

41

operators were having so much trouble picking up the spot at which she must inevitably enter.

Finally she emerged, and the fans did their collective nut. So ecstatic was her reception that it was obvious the performance she was about to deliver had already been taken as read, so there was no real reason why she shouldn't have turned around and gone home again—especially considering that the tail end of her coat, composed of the pelts of innumerable small animals, had undoubtedly not yet left the dressing-room. But she had much to give, and proceeded to give it, making it obvious from the first bar that 40 years away from Germany had done nothing to re-jig the vowels which first intrigued the world in the English language-version of *The Blue Angel*.

'I get no kick in a plen,' she announced. 'Flying too highee with a guyee in the skyee/Is my idea of nothing to do.' Equally, mere alcahall didn't thrill her at ol. Any lingering doubts that such sedulously furbished idiosyncrasy is an acceptable substitute for singing were annihilated by the tumult which greeted each successive rendition, the brouhaha being reinforced at key points by a lissom shedding of the pelts and a line of patter marked by those interminable coy pauses which in the world of schlock theatre are known as 'timing', although they have little to do with skill and everything to do with a celebrity using prestige as leverage.

As the great lady went on recounting the story of her life in song and anecdote, the sceptical viewer was torturing himself with the premonition that there might never be an end. There was, though—although the final number was only the beginning of it, there being a convention in this branch of theatre that the star takes twice as long to get off as she does to get on. It was at this point that the floral tributes started hitting the stage, to the lady's overmastering astonishment: perhaps she had been expecting them to throw book-tokens. The show threatened to fade on the spectacle of these epicene maniacs bombarding her with shrubbery, but as the curtains closed and the applause dipped she paged the tabs with a practised sweep of the arm and emerged to milk dry the audience's last resources of pious energy. If she'd been holding a loaded Luger they couldn't have responded more enthusiastically. They had no choice.

7 January, 1973

Likely lads

SEQUELS are rarely as strong as the originals, but *Whatever Happened to the Likely Lads?* (BBC1) is currently breaking the rule. The lines are acted out with engaging clumsiness by Rodney Bewes as Bob and James Bolam as Terry. With his large featureless head, Bob is the perfect visual complement for Terry, who has a small set of headless features: the chums can fluff, miss cues and just plain forget without even once looking like strangers to each other. But it's the writing that stars: Dick Clement and Ian la Frenais are plainly having a wonderful time raiding their own memories. Rilke once said that no true poet minds going to jail, since it leaves him alone to plunder his treasure-house. Writing this series must be the next best thing to being slung in the chokey.

Back from the forces, Terry has spent the last couple of months trying to pull the birds. Bob, however, is on the verge of the ultimate step with the dreaded Thelma, and last week felt obliged to get rid of his boyhood encumbrances. Out of old tea-chests came the golden stuff: Dinky toys, Rupert and Picturegoer Annuals, all the *frisson*-inducing junk that Thelma would never let weigh down the shelf-units. 'I need these for reference,' whined Bob, with his arms full of cardboard-covered books. There were Buddy Holly 78s –

never called singles in those days, as Terry observed with the
fanatical pedantry typical of the show. Obviously Bob will
have a terrible time with Thelma.

Just as obviously his friendship with Terry will never
cease: Damon and Pythias, Castor and Pollux, perhaps even
Butch and Sundance, but never—not in a million years—
Alias Smith and Jones (BBC2), which is typical American
TV in that the buddies have no past.

11 March, 1972

Nixon on the skids

WITH a breathtaking surge of technology, pencil-thin
beams of ozone-fresh oscillation soared into the night
sky above the wind-scoured Atlantic, bounced off the
vacuum-cradled skin of a communications satellite, speared
downward through the rain-drenched darkness enshrouding
England, tripped the ball-cock of a Baird colour television
receiver and flushed the face of *Richard Nixon* into my living-
room. And what do you know, he was *still* selling himself.
'There can be no whitewash', he announced with a husky
quaver of anguished conviction, 'at the White House.'

The BBC had a couple of early-morning hours to fill
before Nixon's face was ready for transmission. They pre-
luded the event with some interesting programmes beamed
from America and some less interesting acts chosen from the
local pundit-farm. As well as the CBS News, starring Walter
Cronkite, there was an American programme compiling
interview footage of Truman, Eisenhower, Kennedy,
Johnson and Nixon. The level of intelligence was high: even
I was glad to see, from Eisenhower—the only modern
President, it has always seemed, who sincerely wanted less
power than the office affords.

Our own resources of expertise were necessarily less exalted, although Peregrine Worsthorne had managed to make the scene and was eager to express his hope that Nixon would get out of the spot he was in, thereby restoring the authority of the Presidential office and ensuring the safety of the Free World. An American on the panel tried to remind him that the way to restore authority to the Presidential office would be to find out the truth about the man currently holding it, rather than perpetuate a cover-up.

For some reason the point was pursued no further, and I wasn't able to tell whether Perry had commenced grappling with this new view of the problem. He must have been working on it at some level of his complex intellect, however, because about 2·7 seconds after Nixon had finished speaking he was calling the speech 'ominous' and declaring his titanic disillusionment. Like Beethoven crossing Napoleon's name off the 'Eroica', Perry was a study in tottering idealism and god-like scorn. The tube fairly trembled.

But throughout the week, in all the programmes devoted to this issue, there were the odd notes of realism — and realism, one is convinced, is still the stuff to cling to while the ideologists on both wings act out their fantasies. On *This Week* (Thames) there was a rather marvellous lady who had the low-down on Ron Ziegler and company. 'These people', she declared with a yelp of delight, 'have been selling soap for years!' If anybody still wants to know what freedom means, the way she spoke is what it means.

6 May, 1973

Harry Commentator

BY a tragic fluke of inattention I missed the immortal moment when Frank Bough said, 'Harry Commentator is your carpenter,' but otherwise this reporter was in close attendance on most of the week's detritus, miscalculation and trivia. The only serious omission was one's failure to watch Ludovic Kennedy conducting *The U-Boat War* (BBC1).

Usually one likes to be on hand when Kennedy is sinking units of the German Navy, to catch that elegiac stiff lower register when he intones over *Scharnhorst*'s or *Bismarck*'s imminent departure for the bottom of the Atlantic. Bubbles of fuel oil come up, mountains of metal go down, and by now the Kriegsmarine is wearing thin. The subs are surely the fag-end of the subject. But the Japanese, be it remembered, had plenty of capital ships: in my recollection Kennedy hasn't yet sunk a single one of them. There's no reason why the perennial scenario shouldn't be trotted out once, or even thrice, again.

Anyhow, back to business. On *Cup Final* (BBC1) the Duchess of Kent seemed to be rendering her own version, delivered sideways to a companion, of 'Abide With Me'. As far as I could tell from reading her enchanting lips, it took the form of an uninterrupted stream of chat. Her rendition of 'God Save the Queen', on the other hand, stuck close to the original.

Among the preliminaries to the match was a foot-race, undoubtedly staged so that the BBC could bring to an apogee of perfection its age-old pretence of traumatised astonishment at David Bedford coming second. The match itself yielded little of interest apart from football. The carpentry was remarkably restrained, only rising to the exalted heights we expect from David Coleman when Leeds's

Madeley ran flat-out into Sunderland's Guthrie and jolted him sideways out of his jock-strap like a rogue truck uprooting a parking meter. 'Interesting watching that challenge by Madeley.'

Later in the week, on *Sportsnight* (BBC1), the boys were back to form. Some of the Russian gymnasts had been brought over by the British Amateur Gymnastics Association, which concerns itself with amateur gymnastics, and the *Daily Mirror*, which concerns itself with professional money-making. Considering this disparity, it was remarkable how the *Daily Mirror*'s name sprang to prominence in both the camera-work and the carpentry.

Tourischeva re-established her ascendancy: her beautiful programme on the asymmetric bars has the mature inevitability we have so far missed in the work of the more spectacular Olga Korbut. Olga was there too, the sound-waves of the BBC's hysterical build-up still raging around her pretty head. She was on rotten form. The gems from Francis Lai that were emanating from a very bad piano – played, with matching skill, by persons unknown – trickled to a halt when, or perhaps just before, Olga mucked up her back flip on the beam. She also goofed on the asymmetric bars, so it was not surprising to hear Alan Weeks get to the heart of the matter with his usual epigrammatic precision. 'That', he crooned, 'was Olga Korbut at her best.' He would have said the same if she'd flown sideways off the bars and landed head first in the carpentry box.

13 May, 1973

Eddie Waring communicates

ON *Z Cars* (BBC1) a lady answered all our prayers by crowning Sgt Haggar with a bottle. Hip Warboys nailed straight-arrow Taylor on the ITV tennis series, a disguised cigarette ad calling itself the JOHN PLAYER TROPHY. The BBC, not to be outdone, faithfully telecast cricket results in the JOHN PLAYER LEAGUE.

If TV channels are going to make programmes from sponsored events, they might as well just allow sponsored programmes and quit being coy. Direct sponsorship is less corrupting, if cornier. In Australia once a commentator described how a famous batsman had just been run out, promised that the batsman was on his way to the microphone to have a chat, and filled the intervening half-minute with an hysterical encomium for the sponsor, Turf cigarettes. When the batsman finally arrived the commentator said loudly: 'Have a Turf.' The batsman said, equally loudly: 'No, thanks, they hurt my throat.'

World in Action (Granada) featured a multi-millionaire with a joke moustache who gave two of his millions to the Nixon compaign because he wanted to be a Part of a Great Man's Life – the bad buy of the century. With its first episode screened out of synch and sliced into optical salami by pre-prepared fadeouts for American commercials, the new Kenneth Clark art series, *Romantic v. Classic Art* (ATV) nevertheless lost no time in revealing itself to be one of the best things yet from television's premier talking head. His elegant, perspicuous sentences proved all over again that telly talk need not necessarily slobber the English language to death with its big, dumb, toothless mouth.

Out of the screen and into your living-room rode horsemen by Delacroix. 'Having **conquered** the civilized world,' Clark enunciated evenly, 'they have no idea of what to do with it: they will destroy it out of sheer embarrassment.' Written like a gentleman. An ad for Dulux managed to worm its way in while Clark was plugging Géricault, but it didn't much confuse the issue. Dulux doesn't sound like a painter – although Géricault, when you think about it, does sound like a paint.

Every week I watch Stuart Hall on *It's A Knock-Out* (BBC1) and realise with renewed despair that the most foolish thing I ever did was to turn in my double-O licence and hand back that Walther PPK with the short silencer. Some poor klutz running flat out on a rolling log with a bucket of Géricault in each hand is trying to spit greased ping-pong balls into a basket held between the knees of a girl team-mate bouncing on a trampoline with her wrists tied behind her back, and Hall is shouting: 'The seconds count, Robert. Are you going to do it? *Are you going to do it?* Ten seconds to go, Robert! Yes, YOU MUST DO IT NOW, because if you don't, you ... OOH! *Will you make it?* AAAGH!'

As trained attendants scoop Robert's remains on to a stretcher, Stuart goes through the adding-up ritual with the dreaded Arthur. 'That's four points from before and two points now,' Arthur announces, supported in his cogitations by Stuart's arm around his shoulders, 'and four and two make ... ' 'Yes, Arthur?' 'Six.'

Cut to Eddie Waring at the marathon, *Knock-Out*'s Augean Stables. 'Ahn eeh ahm da whey,' bellows Eddie, rocking from foot to foot like a man in the early stages of the hully-gully: 'oom wah hoom there's still one more go to game.' Behind him, on a beam over a tank full of water, two shivering comptometer operators slug each other with pillows. The rain pours down.

I, you and millions upon millions of others watch on. *Panem et circenses* for the last Romans. But the divertimenti, thank God, are gladiatorial only in the metaphorical sense:

49

bursting a balloon full of orangeade with your teeth before falling head-first into a barrel of flour is a lot better than a poke in the eye with a burnt trident.

17 June, 1973

Kinds of freedom

THE pace was a cracker when fifteen elongated sweeties settled down for the final stretch of the race to acquire Zoe Spink's crown as *Miss TV Times 73* (Thames), a bauble which carries with it riches unknown to the Moguls of Ind: a £500 cheque, a luxury holiday in Greece and £200-worth of Woolmark fashion garments, not to mention the bon-bons which every finalist gets as a matter of course — a Molmax Ferrari tote-bag, a Mary Quant 'overnighter' beauty pack and a Braemar fully-fashioned sweater in superwash wool.

With such a radiant crock at the end of the rainbow, it was no wonder that the contestants were so high-powered. Miss ATV Midland, Pamela Calver, was not only lovely, she was interested in karate and sketching. Miss Granada, Marcelline Dixon, in addition to her mind-watering beauty had the attribute of being interested in walking. There was something restfully cultivated about that — one conjured the image of a Renaissance lady rustling through the gloom of a Michelozzo cloister on her way to turn down the advances of a minor Petrarchist and so get herself immortalised in a sonnet-cycle. Miss Channel, Brenda Haldane, on the other hand, established even more striking connotations of thoughtful leisure: she was interested in sunbathing.

With a field ranging all the way from a graphics-orientated athlete whose hands were deadly weapons to an island-dwelling contemplative who just lay there, it would have been a foolish man who jumped to conclusions about which girl was destined to superwash that fully-fashioned sweater in the luxury hotel-room on Corfu. The tests were fierce: no sooner had the prescribed walk in swimming togs and platform shoes been negotiated (Miss Granada scoring heavily here) than the girls were pitch-forked into a blistering Socratic dialogue with Pete Murray, briefed to probe for and lay bare the poise and personality of the girl fit to take over Zoe's crown. It was somewhere about here that the whole show suddenly went ape.

As far as I can recall through the hangover induced by trying to drown the memory of the scene I am now attempting to evoke, each girl was turned loose in Madame Tussaud's and asked to cuddle up to the effigy of the man she admired most. The results were bizarre beyond credibility. One girl's choice nonplussed even the veteran Murray. Why *that* statue in particular? Because he, piped the lass, had all the qualities she'd like in a man. You have to believe me when I tell you that she had her arms around Henry VIII.

Australia's cracker-barrel pixie, Richard Neville, had a show to himself called *A Kind of Freedom* (ATV) in which he returned to the You Beaut Country to do it the favour of contrasting its uptight mores with his own liberated personality. I have known and liked Richard Neville for years and believe him to be a true innocent, whose responsibility for the unique combination of narrow-eyed opportunism and cretinous fantasising which goes on amongst his entourage is strictly limited by a feel for politics that never got beyond the problems involved in sharing out the Dinky Toys before playing in the sandpit.

'Man is only fully free when he plays,' Neville announced in this programme, 'it's his most creative and unpsychotic state.' You have to be a child to believe that, and the time is approaching at a rate of knots when the love generation will no longer be credible as children.

Dotted here and there through the show were phrases

indicating that Neville has all he needs to be a writer –
except, of course, respect for writing. But mostly the script
was radical cheek. Cars were 'twentieth-century gods'. A
supermarket was 'a shining edifice of drudgery'. You name
it and he had a cliché for it. At one point he was to be
found blaming our 'corrupt value system' for his own
stardom.

There was the odd good thing. He waxed envious about
the surfies; having been, like me, a couple of years too late
to catch their wave. Where we had the leaden arms of the
body-surfer, the surfies had Malibu boards and the balletic
lightness of a musculature dedicated to balancing on top of
the Pacific Ocean instead of bullocking through it. It was a
real revolution, bringing with it a pantheistic grace that left
the previous generation clutching its life-saving medals in a
rictus of jealousy. The effort I put into winning three Bronze
Medallions has left me with a grudge against society and
wrists that trail along the ground.

On such a subject Neville had something to say and said
it with engaging tentativeness. On most subjects he had
nothing to say and said it with a babbling fluency that made
you wonder if perhaps he hadn't popped a hinge. All too
symbolically, the show wound up with Louise and Richard
doffing their clobber and disappearing among rocky outcrops
shrouded by the mist of a waterfall. That was the revolution,
folks – cool as a mountain stream.

Harlech set fire to a hill of money in an effort to capture
the putative magic of the Fabulous Burtons (*Divorce His,
Divorce Hers*) and although the John Hopkins script was
more realistic than usual in its dialogue (if no less unintelli-
gible in its time-scale) the show declined to become airborne.
But after movies as monumentally lousy as *Bluebeard* and
Hammersmith is Out it was good to see Burton chipping some
of the rust off his technique. 'Beat me black and blue but
please don't leave me,' chirped Taylor, doing her best to
believe in the role. Her hair was by Alexandre of Paris, and

the two-part programme was shot in those well-known Welsh mining communities Munich and Rome.

1 July, 1973

Blue-bloods on parade

SIR Alec Douglas-Home, the current incarnation of an earldom marching out of the far past on its way to the far future, had a *Panorama* (BBC1) all to himself. Fully equipped with knuckle-dusters, bother-boots and a fountain-pen loaded with nitric acid, I was all set to be objective about this programme, but in a kinky way it turned out to be kind of winning. Sir Alec saw politics 'as a public service rather than a means to exercise power.' Expanding on this point, he said that he saw politics as a public service rather than a means to exercise power. Or to put it another way, it was public service, rather than power, that interested him most in politics. Power was a thing to be eschewed: in politics, public service was what really mattered.

On the vexed question of the young Sir Alec's academic attainments, his Oxford tutor was ready with a pithy summary: 'He was interested in people and events.' But dons are nothing if not precise in their language, and a few moments later came the qualifier by which judgment was subtly enriched. 'He was interested in events and he was interested in people.'

Out in the Tory grassroots, the constituents were less guarded in their praise – especially the ladies. 'Ah admah him because of his complete honestah and sinceritah.' The ancestral lands, incorporating the River Tweed, rolled on as far as the ravished eye could see. Sir Alec's success in brushing off the calumny of a scornful world, one reflected, might possibly have something to do with possessing such a large amount of it in which to retreat.

Lady Antonia Fraser had *One Pair of Eyes* (BBC2) and – if you'll forgive the male chauvinist piggery – very nice eyes they were. If you could concentrate on them while ignoring the programme, you had a chance of retaining consciousness throughout. If you couldn't, then the evening tended towards narcosis. The besotted director seemed suicidally intent on demonstrating Lady Antonia's versatility: shots of Lady Antonia walking were succeeded by shots of Lady Antonia talking, these in turn giving way to a virtuoso passage of Lady Antonia walking and talking simultaneously. Already stunned, the viewer was in no condition to remain unmoved when the screen suddenly erupted with the image of Lady Antonia typing.

Lady Antonia was of the opinion, which the producer unaccountably encouraged her to deliver over and over while the scenery was changed around her, that biography is of central importance in the study of history. A friend, Christopher Falkus, found a way of putting it less memorably. 'One of the tremendously ... *corny* things one can say about a novel', he said, 'is that it has a beginning, a middle and an end. One can say the same thing about a biography.' Lady Antonia nodded agreement – as well she might, the point being irrefutable.

Climax of the show was some tomfool reconstruction of a dramatic escape from a castle, with the part of Mary Queen of Scots being taken by Lady Antonia whose viewpoint was represented by a hand-held camera. As the flurry of fancy editing subsided, Lady Antonia blushingly explained that the escape had not been real, but had been staged by the BBC: plainly she was worried lest we identify too closely with the action. She herself found it difficult not to identify with Mary Queen of Scots. 'I also have a house on an island in Scotland,' she confessed, 'but not shut away. Rather the reverse.'

Similarly well-bred, Andrew Robert Buxton Cavendish,

Duke of Devonshire (*The World of the Eleventh Duke*, BBC1)
shared Lady Antonia's upper-class singularities of diction –
particuly in his confidently elliptical approach to those
words where some attempt to pronounce the constituent
consonants is populy supposed to be mandatory – but
differed in possessing an ability to blend into the scenery like
a chameleon. There is nothing to say about him except that
Chatsworth is the most beautiful estate the mind of man can
imagine and that he is eminently qualified to maintain it. If
the place were nationalised tomorrow, he'd have to be hired
to look after it, although perhaps at a slightly reduced
stipend. Don Haworth's script was a witty job which Derek
Hart spoke like a gentleman. The decisive gulf separating the
duke from his horny-palmed employees, in my view, is that
while they wear baggy clothes bought off the hook, his
baggy clothes are tailor-made.

8 and 22 July, 1973

Squire Hadleigh

A MONARCH operating within understood limits,
Hadleigh (Yorkshire) is the perfect squire, paternalisti-
cally careful of his tenantry's welfare, beloved in the village,
respected in the council, savage with the stupid, gentle with
the helpless, gorgeous in his hand-made threads. In the
current series, which in my house is watched with a pre-
tence of scornful detachment somewhat nullified by the size
of the bribes offered our elder child to hit the sack before
it starts, Hadleigh has taken to himself a wife, played by
Hilary Dwyer – one of those leggy jobs with Botticelli
shoulders and no bra.

Hadleigh himself is the British imperialist up to his old
colonial tricks on the soil of home: the palaver with the

tenants is pure Sanders of the River, and when he sets about correcting a local injustice it's Bulldog Drummond Attacks. Just on his own, Hadleigh encapsulates the modern male dream of the cool aristo. Gerald Harper has oodles of athletic zip (his imitation of a horse in the Jean-Louis Barrault *Rabelais* at the Roundhouse was the only interesting thing in that entire weary evening) and a mannerist voice that issues in a succession of resonant simpers and shouts from an identikit aquiline profile in which the features of everybody from Leslie Howard in *Pimpernel Smith* to Stewart Granger as Beau Brummell are eerily conflated. You could guarantee ten million viewers on the strength of Harper alone.

The other seven million (yes, *seventeen million* people watch this thing) are doubtless ensnared by the cunning stroke of calculation which gives Mrs Hadleigh a lower-class background. She has been saved from drudgery by a knight in a shining white V8 Aston Martin; and then again, she has qualities that the dollies born to the purple perhaps do not possess; and besides, who but the beautiful deserve the brave?

Rounding out the dream world is their body-servant, Sutton. Silent, omni-competent, his only ambition to serve his master until and beyond death, he brings Hadleigh messages on a silver salver while you and I pass each other the thin mints without taking our hungry eyes from the screen. *Hadleigh* is the last, plush gasp of the old England – a purgative draught of nostalgia which one sincerely trusts will leave its army of viewers fresh to do battle in the real world. Which is the world where the squires are dead or dying and the tailors are chalking suits for property developers.

19 August, 1973

Drained crystals

ON *Star Trek* (BBC1) our galaxy got itself invaded from a parallel universe by an alien *Doppelgänger* toting mysterioso weaponry. These bad vibes in the time-warp inspired the line of the week. 'Whatever that phenomenon was,' piped Kirk's dishy new black lieutenant, 'it drained our crystals almost completely. Could mean trouble.'

In our house for the past few years it's been a straight swap between two series: if my wife is allowed to watch *Ironside* I'm allowed to watch *Star Trek*, and so, by a bloodless compromise possible only between adults, we get to watch one unspeakable show per week each. (My regular and solitary viewing of *It's a Knock-Out* and *Mission Impossible* counts as professional dedication.)

How, you might ask, can anyone harbour a passion for such a crystal-draining pile of barbiturates as *Star Trek*? The answer, I think, lies in the classical inevitability of its repetitions. As surely as Brünnhilde's big moments are accompanied by a few bars of the Valkyries' ride, Spock will say that the conclusion would appear to be logical, captain. Uhura will turn leggily from her console to transmit information conveying either (a) that all contact with Star Fleet has been lost, or (b) that it has been regained. Chekhov will act badly. Bones ('Jim, it may seem unbelievable, but my readings indicate that this man has ... *two hearts*') will act extremely badly. Kirk, employing a thespian technique picked up from someone who once worked with somebody who knew Lee Strasberg's sister, will lead a team consisting of Spock and Bones into the *Enterprise*'s transporter room and so on down to the alien planet on which the Federation's will is about to be imposed in the name of freedom.

The planet always turns out to be the same square mile of rocky Californian scrubland long ago overexposed in the

Sam Katzman serials: Brick Bradford was there, and Captain Video – not to mention Batman, Superman, Jungle Jim and the Black Commando. I mean like this place has been *worn smooth*, friends. But the futuristic trio flip open their communicators, whip out their phasers, and peer alertly into the hinterland, just as if the whole lay-out were as threateningly pristine as the Seven Cities of Cibola. *Star Trek* has the innocence of belief.

It also has competition. On the home patch, an all-British rival has just started up. Called *Moonbase 3* (BBC1), it's a near-future space opera plainly fated to run as a serial, like *Dr Who*, rather than as a series. In this way it will avoid the anomalies – which I find endearing – that crop up when one self-contained *Star Trek* episode succeeds another. In a given episode of the *Enterprise*'s voyages (Its Mission: To Explore Strange New Worlds) the concept of parallel universes will be taken for granted. In the next episode, the possibility will be gravely discussed. Such inconsistencies are not for *Moonbase 3*, which after one instalment has already turned out to possess the standard plot of the bluff new commander setting out to restore the morale of a shattered unit: i.e., *Angels One Five* or *Yangtze Incident* plus liquid oxygen.

Moonbases 1 and 2 belong to the United States and the U.S.S.R. Moonbase 3 belongs to Europe, so it looks like ELDO got into orbit after all. Being European, the base's budget is low, but its crew can supply zest and colour when aroused. The ambitious second-in-command, Lebrun, says things like 'Zoot' to prove that he is French. The in-house quack, Dr Smith, is a lushly upholstered young lady with a grape-pulp mouth who is surely destined to drain the new commander's crystals at an early date.

In the revived *Softly, Softly* (BBC1), Harry the Hawk leapt back to form by cocking up within the first ten minutes, thereby opening the way for a sequence of pithy sermons from Frank Windsor. The Hawk externalised his frustrations in the usual manner, opening and closing every door in sight. Evans has lost two stone and Snow has now reached the final stage of *angst*-ridden taciturnity, staring at his superiors like Diogenes when Alexander blocked the sun. The dirigible-sized question hanging over the series is whether Barlow will return.

Spy Trap (BBC1) is back, but Commander Anderson has moved on, being replaced by a narrow-eyed wonder-boy called Sullivan, who in the first episode successively penetrated HQ's security, uncovered Commander Ryan's secret, tortured a heavy and ripped off the cap of a ball-point with his teeth.

One of those BBC2 link-men, specially chosen for their inability to get through a typewritten line of the English language without fluffing, announced 'another in this series of nothing ventured, nothing win adventures starring noo, nah, George Plimpton.'

The male voice-over on the new Make-a-Meal commercial said: 'If you're a woman you're a meal-maker for someone.' Keep a hand over your crystals, brother: if a women's libber catches you they'll be drained for sure. One of the art directors on the old Vincent Price movie *The Fly* (ITV) bore the name Theobold Holsopple. Beat that.

16 September, 1973

Anne and Mark get married

NIGGLE as they might through the days leading up to the main event, the iconoclasts cut little ice.

Switching on *The Frost Show* (LWT) late, as part of my usual preparation for switching it off early, I found Alan Brien declaring that it was nonsense to treat the Royals as something special and that what he had recently done for

Anne he would have done for any girl—i.e., travel to Kiev and position himself beside a difficult fence in order to describe her as bandy-legged when she fell off her horse. Angus Maude, M.P., then gave the hapless Brien what small assistance he still needed in alienating the audience's sympathies, and with a healthy sigh of anticipation we entered the period of curfew, or purdah: from here until lift-off the tone would be affirmative, *nem. con.* It was hard to see why this should not be so. Though nobody out there in the videospace knew very much about Anne's personality or anything at all about Mark's, the wish to see them properly spliced was surely very widely shared.

On the Monday night the BBC and ITV both screened the same interview with the betrothed twain. Andrew Gardner, wearing the discreet grin and the cheery twinkle, represented commercial television. Alastair Burnet, wearing the awe-stricken pallor and the beatified smile, incarnated the spirit of Establishment broadcasting. The Princess immediately proceeded to run deeply incised rings around both of them. Anne, it was suddenly apparent, was perfectly at ease, more than a tinge larky, smart as a whip and not disposed to suffer fools gladly. To help her prove this last point, Gardner and Burnet did everything but dress up in cap and bells: whether because their lines of inquiry had previously been checked and vetted into inanity, or because both had fallen prey to a shattering attack of *folie à deux*, they served up questions the like of which had not been heard before in the history of the human race. It was a mercy when an embarrassing point was abandoned so that a fatuous one might be taken up.

Anne had an opinion on everything except the political role of the monarchy—an understandable lacuna. Mark's views were not so easily elicited. Here was Beatrice, but where was Benedick? Still, Benedick himself had been a stumbler for love: for these fellows of infinite tongue, that can rhyme themselves into ladies' favours, they do always reason themselves out again. Much more inhibiting was the problem of impersonal speech: second nature to Anne, it was as yet an obstacle to Mark, who had still to grasp the principle that the whole art of making oneself understood when one is confining onself to the one pronoun is just to bash on regardless even when one's ones threaten to overwhelm one. His shy charm there was no denying, although the piercing Colortran lights gave him blushes that were younger than his years. The theme by which his life was linked to hers, it inexorably emerged, was horses. From this rich deposit of equine subject-matter, one guessed, would exfoliate much of the media-men's symbolism on the magic day. And so, with a head full of Piesporter fumes and the first bars of the overture to a Wagnerian dose of flu, your reporter flamed out into the flea-bag.

The Day dawned over Islington in the form of a flawless canopy of *pietra serena* rubbed with crushed roses – a spectacle which gradually transmuted itself into the palest of pure Wedgwood as one fed a hot lemon drink to one's throat-load of streptococci. The Beeb led off with the official photos and a daring, jauntily suitable use of the Beatles' 'When I'm 64'. Fyffe Robertson was on hand, reading with undiminished verve from what might possibly have been a steam-powered autocue. *Nationwide* reporters were everywhere among the citizenry. Asked how tall she thought Anne was, a little girl guessed 3 ft. Ursula Bloom, purportedly the author of 500 books, and lately the perpetrator of something called *Princesses in Love*, gave an interview in which it was pretty thoroughly established that Anne is good with animals. Astrologers were called in: Anne's Fourth Node was in the Fifth House of Creative Love so the whole deal was already sewn up tight, no sweat. A woman had been to 10,000 weddings.

At 8 a.m. Alastair Burnet came on, still radiating a nimbus while dutifully flogging the tone of portent. 'And no doubt, if the bride is awake and has peeped out through the curtains ... ,' he speculated tweely. Valerie Singleton promised

that in the course of the next hour we would be shown what
the dress might look like, to tide us over the further two hours
before we would be shown what the dress did actually look
like. Another astrologer gratuitously proclaimed that Mark
wasn't as dreary and ineffectual as one might imagine – Leo
and Virgo had complementary strengths. Bob Wellings
talked to Mark's tank crew. 'Is he, is he, does he, is he ...
popular?' 'Yes.' Film of Mark protruding staunchly from the
reverse-parked turret of a Chieftain belting along a road in
Germany indicating that Virgo came not unarmed to the
combat with Leo.

Valerie Singleton talked to Richard Meade. Meade
alleged, sensationally, that Mark was very shy. In Belfast,
Mr and Mrs Monahan were interviewed. Married for
seventy years, they were as sweet-natured as they were
unintelligible. Burnet chaired a discussion with some Miss
World contestants. My compatriot, Miss Australia, the
current title-holder, ventured intrepidly into the nether levels
of depth-psychology: 'I think, arm, it must be a nerve-racking
experience for both of them.' 'I oper,' said Miss Belgium, 'I
oper we will be seeing it on Belgian television.' She could rest
assured: 500 million people would be plugged in by the time
the real action started.

Alison Oliver, Anne's trainer, was interviewed up-country.
'What's the atmosphere like before a big event?' Mrs Oliver
explained persuasively that it could be quite tense. At 9 a.m.
Pete Murray was shown coaxing record requests from people
lining the route. A bystander, Julie Granchip, thought the
wedding was great, and the reason she was here was to see
the wedding, because the wedding, she thought, would be
great. 'Julie, thanks for talking to us.'

To the West Country, where Mark's village, Great
Somerford, has slept through the centuries awaiting its
encounter with Cliff Michelmore. The local bell-ringers
thought the programme of 5,000-odd changes scheduled
for the Abbey was a breeze: they aimed to double it. 'You're

goana doublet?' bellowed Cliff, 'I doan believe ya.' The Red Arrows performed to the music of Buddy Rich – the most gripping imagery of the morning.

'A lot of people, perhaps,' intoned Burnet, 'are wondering why Captain Phillips is not the Earl of Somerford.' The Richmond Herald said that a title had been withheld for political reasons. Richmond, you could see, thought that democracy was getting out of hand. In the Abbey the carpets had been cleaned and covered with druggets. The druggets were being cleaned.

Michele Brown talked to a little girl. Why was she here? 'Wedding.' 'Japan', said a Japanese, 'has a loyal famiry rike you have.' Too tlue. A résumé, in stills and film, of Mark's career, showing how he rode before he could walk. One got the impression that he had trampled the midwife.

'Do you think she's a typical young girl?' Michele Brown asked a typical young girl. 'No.' 'Do you think she's got too many privileges?' 'Yes.' 'What privileges?' 'Horses.' Anne Monsarrat, a mine of royal information, told us that James I's daughter had had the most expensive gown and that Henrietta Maria's train had a man underneath it. Dimbling suavely, Tom Fleming introduced the scene in the Abbey and environs. 'And here is the bride's home ...' he jested, over a shot of Buckingham Palace. 'Perhaps he's there in spirit ... ' he conjectured, over a shot of George VI's statue. Fleming flanneled devotedly for some time, being particularly careful, in the early stages, to keep us in ignorance of who the guests shown to be arriving might in fact be. Janey Ironside extemporised a commentary, with mixed results, on the range of hats available. It was a suitable time for the bored viewer to switch over to ITV, discover it to be screening a Profile of Princess Anne, and switch back again. The Household Cavalry rode out of the Palace gates. 'For a bride and groom who have an interest in horses,' ventured Fleming, 'this must be a thrilling sight.' Mark's parents arrived at the Abbey. 'A few weeks ago,' announced

Fleming, with that peculiar combination of awe and vulgarity which the BBC needs so acutely to be rid of, 'people might have said, who are *they*?'

Blues, Royals ... Glass Coach! She was on the way. Cut back to the Abbey, where Mark stood poised before the altar – the final fence for a clear round. What did Stendhal say about the novel, that it's a mirror going down a road? The British Constitution is a Princess going down an aisle. As the Dean and the Archbishop begin to read their text, the prattle of the media-men perforce ceases, and for a while the resplendent poetry of the marriage service lifts the proceedings beyond the grasp of straining hacks, before the demented chanting and the kapok-voiced lesson-reading of the minor clerics haul it back down to drugget-level.

No less buoyant than its hallowed cargo's hearts, the Glass Coach spins back to the Palace, where Fleming's voice awaits them with the completion of the week's recurring theme. 'I'm sure', he sings, 'these horses know that they're home.'

18 November, 1973

Just call me 'Captain'

AND in a moment, *Crossroads*, and a new guest on Vera's houseboat! But first, the show that came out of nowhere to establish itself overnight as the laugh riot of 1973 – *Cudlipp and be Damned*. Billed as BBC1's Tuesday Documentary, this miracle of unrelieved adoration was in fact a pioneering amalgam of slack-jawed piety and sophisticated urban humour, yielding merriment by the crystal bucket.

A lawyer, Mr Ellis Birk, set the general tone of the programme, and the specific intensity of his own future contributions to it, by leading off with the ringing assertion that

Hugh Cudlipp was 'the greatest tabloid journalist of all time'. It was hard to still a wicked interior voice which insisted on pointing out that this was tantamount to calling a man the greatest manufacturer of potato-pistols who had ever lived, or the greatest salesman of sticky sweets in the history of dentistry. Nevertheless such a naughty itch required ruthlessly to be suppressed. Anyone aware of what tabloid journalism has become since the *Mirror*'s heyday, and of what tabloid journalism generally consisted of *during* the *Mirror*'s heyday, will hasten to assert that Cudlipp ran an outstanding newspaper of its type – he backed good causes and appealed to the best side of the common people. With that said, however, one doesn't feel bound to convey the impression that Hugh Cudlipp is Proust. The programme did feel bound to convey that, and that he was Balzac, Tolstoy, Flaubert, Dostoevsky and Henry James.

One had written off as a coincidence the revelation that Mr Ellis Birk, chorus-master of the hosannahs, is currently employed by the organisation of which the *uomo universale* he so admires is the chief. But the number of such coincidences quickly mounted, as people figuring prominently on Cudlipp's payroll rushed forward to say how wonderful he was. Marjorie Proops came on, deep in the throes of a transfigurative ecstasy, as though St Teresa had once again been pierced through and through by the spear of Christ. 'He makes my adrenalin ... ' But she couldn't think of exactly what it was that Hugh Cudlipp made her adrenalin do. Boil? Curdle? One thing she was clear about: his merest summons engendered in her bosom – this she clutched – a delicious cocktail of excitement and fear.

The theme of fear was touched upon by all contributors. Plainly the idea that his striding advent among their toiling backs made even the most hardened of his bond-men oscillate with trepidation was one that went down a bomb with the boss. That it had a similar appeal for Ivan the Terrible was not among the points raised. The concept being peddled was one of benevolent despotism, in which Hugh brought out the best in these marvellously talented people by putting the fear of God into them. Donald Zec had something to add on this point: an elaborate aria, exquisitely sung, of orgasmic power-worship.

Lest Zec and the other dedicated minions had failed to get the message over with the force appropriate to the greatest tabloid journal of all time, the greatest tabloid journalist of all time was asked for his opinion on his own capacity to inspire terror. Eroding a cigar with a mouth whose craggy structure betokened all the firmness of somebody who hasn't been contradicted in several decades, he spake. 'I see no reason for not expressing an opinion rather bluntly.' Bootless to add that a paternalistic twinkle was not far from his eyes: though he loved his paper most, he loved his sweating children near as much. Bootless also to add – or at least Desmond Wilcox, the eerily quiescent linkman, found it so – that the average employee almost invariably finds himself with an excellent reason for not bluntly expressing his own opinion back. The reason being, that whereas the employer can fire the employee, the employee is not in the same position with regard to the employer.

But Cudlipp, we could be assured, though he might be a hard taskmaster, or even a martinet, was no Bourbon. He was a man of the people, a socialist in the true sense – a socialist deep down where it counted, under the meaningless trappings of power and, well, wealth. A salary of £33,000 a year was mentioned, and it was not suggested that his television interests ran at a loss. Roll it together and it made quite a bundle. Doubly a wonder, then, that his democratic ease with ordinary mortals had never left him. His chauffeur calls him 'Hugh'. Rank, we were told, isn't important to him. On his yacht, for example, it is merely necessary to call him 'Captain'. That's the heartwarming thing about democratic leaders: all you have to do is call them something like 'Your Excellency' and they relax completely.

The day Cecil King got the chop was the saddest of Cudlipp's life. Cudlipp said this himself, and his sincerity was patent. Ellis Birk, attaining by now the epigrammatic fluency of a Machiavelli clapping eyes for the first time on Cesare Borgia, said that nobody had ever suffered as Cudlipp suffered that day. Wilcox, rallying from his coma, tried to probe here—why was it that Cudlipp had not delivered the killing stroke in person? Because he could not bear to, out of the love he bore his old mentor. However much the circumstances cried out for the blow, Cudlipp could not plunge the knife into King's chest. So he plunged it into King's back. All the conspirators save only he, you see, did what they did in *envy* of great Caesar.

On New Year's Eve Cudlipp will retire, but we could take it for granted—and if we couldn't, we were reminded of it repeatedly—that his presence will still be felt. Considering his success in getting an entire BBC documentary consecrated exclusively to an oratorio in his praise, there was indeed good cause to think that his energies were ascending to a whole new plateau. It was the self-promotion coup of the year, and one strove in vain to think of anyone else who could have brought it off. On the Street of Adventure there is still only one true whizz-kid.

3 December, 1973

Earthshrinker

'TONIGHT,' said the commercial, 'we'd like to reassure you about the future of coal in this country.'

Since the combined costs of making the commercial and putting it on the screen would have by themselves gone some way towards supplying the miners' demands, the reassurance wasn't all that reassuring, and merely added to the air of unreality the tube has for weeks been busily projecting.

The voice-over sounded as if it might be Patrick Allen, of *Brett* fame – associations there, you see, of entrepreneurial dynamism, and the no-nonsense manliness of such other Allen accounts as Castrol and Wilkinson Sword. He also does Harrods', whose warmth of tone the Coal Board are obviously eager to share.

It's all in how you sell it, especially when a dream is all you've got to sell. Undaunted by the crisis and plainly not to be abashed by anything short of the Last Judgment, the ad-men were still at it full blast, speeding us the good news about such vital resources as Kleenex Boutique (coffee 'n' gold soft petals that fold) and Cadbury's Amazin' (it's Amazin' what raisins can do). Meanwhile, back on BBC1, public service broadcasting was sedulously providing, in the form of a programme called *Holiday 74*, a vision of the consumer society's dreams fully as micro-minded as any mad ad ITV could ever offer.

Holiday 74 begins with half a dozen pairs of knockers swaying, rolling or running at you through varying intensities of exotic sunlight. The emphasis on the untrammelled mammary is kept up throughout, handily symbolising the show's basic assumption that sex is something which happens on holiday. If the soundtrack, speculating on how computer-chosen holiday companions might get on with each other, uses a word like 'compatible', the camera provides a visual reference by panning away abruptly to capture a sun-crazed Aphrodite from Frinton burgeoning wetly from the Aegean, while simultaneously zooming in to snatch a close-up of her flailing barbettes.

Cliff Michelmore, as you might expect, flaunts a grin naughty enough to suit the mood, and adds to the air of spontaneity by reading the autocue as if he had never seen a line of it in his life before. His companion, John Carter, on the other hand, starts off looking very sleepy, perhaps

THE BENDING OF THE SPOONS

desensitised by a clairvoyance of the trivia to come. 'We spend a small fortune in fizzy drinks,' confides a holiday-maker bouncing through Morocco on a bus. The bus is called a Sundecker, to rhyme with the outfit laying the trip on, who call themselves Suntrekker. Apart from the heat — one of the arcana, such as begging, that the alert vacationer must expect to run into in Marrakesh — we could be assured that the Suntrekker Sundecker was the only way to travel. On through dune and wadi it roared, stopping in villages for fizzy drinks: an earth-shrinker.

Cilla (BBC1) was involved in a cretinous routine about Women's Lib, featuring rhymes about women's demand for status, so that they wouldn't have to spend their lives peeling potatus. But her guest, Twiggy, was delightful.

10 January, 1974

The bending of the spoons

IMBUED with the Dunkirk spirit, prominent people are already telling the papers that the restricted telly schedules are not as bad as they expected.

The picture being painted is one of family solidarity and cultural renewal, as husband and wife are released at 10.30 from bondage to the Cyclops, with tons of time to keep that long-delayed appointment with Dostoevsky or load the turn-table with one of those boxed record sets they never previously found time to play.

A sad fact, then, that ITV could have countered BBC2's *Othello* with a screening of the Glyndebourne *Figaro* last Tuesday night if it had not been for early closing. Quite apart from his *Aquarius* activities, Humphrey Burton had previously assured his place in television history by getting an entire evening of ITV's lucrative transmission time devoted, with stunning results, to Verdi's *Macbeth*. With *Figaro* he was all set to work the trick again. But fate intervened, and what did we get instead? Uri Geller (*Is Seeing Believing?* Thames).

I don't mean anything impersonal when I say that Uri is a pain in the neck, not least because of his ability to cream off so much air-time. Magicians hate it when one of their number starts claiming divine powers, for the good reason that they can't discredit him without blowing trade secrets. For this reason, a guru can usually extend his field of operations to the full distance public gullibility will allow. Nor is it certain that the ability to see through such hocus-pocus has much to do with raw I.Q. Conan Doyle was Houdini's mental superior by a mile yet Houdini could never convince Conan Doyle that the spiritualist mediums to whom he gave credence were simply tricksters. Houdini reproduced every spiritualist phenomenon Conan Doyle ever encountered, without changing Conan Doyle's mind by one iota.

The difference between the two men was that Houdini, as a practising illusionist, knew that there could be more to nature than met the eye. Conan Doyle, who severely overrated his own common sense as a speculative instrument, thought that those aspects of nature whose workings weren't immediately apparent to him couldn't be explained without reference to the supernatural. Such a man tends to credit himself with an open mind, when actually his mind is closed to the full variety of life.

Medicine men like Uri can equally count on eager assistance from gormless professors ready to say that Science is Baffled. Scientific method means nothing if it is applied to the wrong problem, and in questions of magic it nearly always is. Transformations, for example, usually depend on working a quick switch, and if the scientific examination is applied to how the material is transformed it will get nowhere, since the only real question is how the magician gets rid of the first object and substitutes the second.

With Uri we're dealing, I think, with a master of misdirection — there can be little doubt that this hectoring shaman is an illusionist of a high order. In addition to his talent, though, he's working under dream conditions. Knowing little about magic — but enough to know a pro when I see one — I can't say how Uri does his stuff: it's for Romark and his fellow tradesmen to say that. But I *can* say that nothing beats a telly studio as a place for a Messiah to work his miracles.

Uri can divert the attention of millions as effectively as if he were sitting in the director's chair. And when he's working in front of a pack of charlies like some of the Thames crew the sky's the limit. Uri can tell the time at least as well as they can, and knows to within a few seconds just when a mag of film is going to run out. What a surprise, then, when he did all that controversial stuff while the poor dopes were changing mags! Here's a bet: the minute a director tells Uri, 'I'm going to keep one camera on your hands and superimpose that image over the programme so that it never leaves the screen,' you'll find that Uri's destiny suddenly calls him elsewhere.

A BBC1 play called *The Lonely Man's Lover*, by Barry Collins, was concerned with harsh change in a tiad landscape. Lizzie (well played by Jan Francis) rejected her destiny as a farm-girl ('We'll need to futtle out them ruddocks before the trunch felths,' said her foster-mother, or words to that effect) and went to live with the famous young poet temporarily second-homing up on the hill. He was identifiable as a poet by his monosyllabic brutishness, although the occasional quotation from his writings was meant to reveal an unsettling command of language: 'We are the reasonable men/The afterbirth of mathematics,' he wrote, thrilling her to the marrow. In due course he confirmed his artistic nature by getting her pregnant and abandoning her, whereupon she returned to the farm ('Get yer boots on and slag that mawk,' etc.), but the old ways had been irreparably broken. One strove to convince oneself that this was a bad thing.

20 January, 1974

More like it

A HIGH-QUALITY Play for Today called *All Good Men* (BBC2) covered familiar ground in an unfamiliar manner. Trevor Griffiths wrote it, and the faultless direction was by Michael Lindsay-Hogg. Venerable Labour politicians who have compromised their early principles are standard stuff (Alan Bennett's *Getting On* is a key text here) but Griffiths has the resources for a fresh look. Bill Fraser was the politico, racked by coronaries on the eve of being elevated to the peerage, scourged by his radical son who believes him to be a class-traitor, and loving a daughter whose love in return has been drained of all admiration.

Into this grim scene wanders Ronald Pickup as an unprincipled telly-man with a Winchester background. He keeps saying 'Ah,' with what the daughter (an altogether excellent performance by Frances de la Tour) calls 'that I'm Not Important style of arrogance.' He's the catalyst for a family explosion, culminating in the son's producing some devastating evidence (echoes of Arthur Miller's *All My Sons* and Ibsen *passim*) that his father had already sold the pass back in 1926.

The son was the most convincing fictional radical to reach the screen in recent times – the kidnappers in this week's edition of the egregious *Barlow* (BBC1) showed you the usual standard – and was played to the hot-eyed hilt by Jack Shepherd. He quoted chapter and verse from *Bury My Heart at Wounded Knee*, unintentionally giving you the sense that Mr Griffiths had been reading that book very recently himself. Influences obtruded throughout the evening. But so did some real writing, and the play got its symbolism over in a single line about squirrels killing a tree by nibbling the bark. Other playwrights please copy.

Such a solid, exploratory and humane effort makes it all the more necessary to declare *The Pallisers* (BBC2) a bit of a dud. I shall watch it through, but without much hope of finding it successful on any level, either as a classic serial or as a Forsyte sudser. Leaving aside the massive pre-emptive publicity, it's a minor event. A lot of money has been put into it, and years of Simon Raven's time, but the acting takes place in the range from minor league to outright inadequate, and the direction only occasionally rises to the uninspired.

Action being thin in Trollope, the author's verbose running commentary is paramount in establishing the characters, such as they are. Bereft of that commentary, his stories don't count for much. Trying to get the characters across without enough dialogue or proper scenes to help them do it, the actors are at sea, and fall back on an all-purpose Period style which is diverting to analyse but tedious to watch in the long run.

I'll come back to this project after a few more episodes, when there is more to bite on. For the moment, there is Burgo's hat, and his cigar, and there is that bloke who in *Z-Cars* plays a detective inspector, and there are pairs of people walking around explaining the plot to each other so that we can overhear, and there is a good deal of racy innuendo from Mr Raven to jazz things up, and there is Susan Hampshire. A lot, an awful lot, depends on whether you go for Susan Hampshire.

My colleague, Tony Palmer, did a documentary on Hugh Hefner, called *The World of Hugh M. Hefner* (Yorkshire). Mocking Hefner is easy to do, and in my view should be made even easier: as editor of *Playboy* and controller of its merchandising empire, he emanates an intensity of solemn foolishness which is no less toxic for calling itself liberating. I would have enjoyed the show more if Palmer had been in love with his subject less. There was a tendency to take the Hefnerite nexus of activities at its self-proclaimed value. Siegfried's Funeral March crashed out heroically on the sound-track where 'My Ding-a-Ling' would have been more appropriate, and the camera drooled like a Pavlov dog as it was led about in Hef's de luxe ambience.

'I live the kind of life surrounded by beautiful things, female and material.' Hefner's use of language was extraordinary. Approving new layouts for the 'What kind of man reads *Playboy*?' series of ads, he said he liked the one 'where the man is showing off the artefact to his date'. Further afield, in such outposts of Hefner's empire as the London Playboy Club, the film-making got more sardonic. There was no gainsaying the fact that to make it as a Bunny a girl needs more than just looks. She needs idiocy, too. Otherwise there'd be no putting up with the callous fatuity of the selection process.

An aspiring Playmate was given a ride in a limousine, and told that she should feel honoured, because being given a ride in a *Playboy* limousine was really exciting. What did she think? 'It's rilly exciting.' Did she feel honoured? 'I rilly do.' We were shown the finer points of the Bunny Dip, which is the technique a waitress uses to bend down without springing out of her wired costume like an auto-inflated life-raft. 'Our notion', averred Hefner, 'was that a total man ought to have a part of his life that could be described as a playboy attitood.' Total Man, showing off the artefact to his date.

3 February, 1974

A pound of flash

ADMIRING Olivier past extravagance, I was little pleased to discover that his Shylock (*The Merchant of Venice*, ATV), infected by the nervous bittiness of the surrounding production, crumbled to the touch.

The British theatre rations itself to one intellectual at a time and currently Jonathan Miller is the one. Being an intellectual is all right by me, and I sincerely hope that Miller will be allowed to go on having ideas until doomsday. It would be nice, though, if his ideas were all as good as most of them are big.

The Big Idea of setting *The Merchant of Venice* in the nineteenth century – apparently to underline the commercial aspects – used itself up in the first few minutes, leaving the viewer to contend with several hours of top-hats, three-piece suits, and bustles. Julia Trevelyan Oman did her usual fanatical-meticulous job in recreating the nineteenth-century Venetian interiors, thereby proving that nineteenth-century Venetian interiors bore a lulling resemblance to nineteenth-century Cromwell Road interiors: a few ceilings-full of reflected water-lights might have made a difference, but strangely they were not forthcoming, so all depended on a quarter of an hour's worth of location footage. It had never been clear in the first place that the nineteenth century was at all an appropriate period in Venetian terms. The city was already far gone in decline by then, and Shakespeare manifestly wrote the play on the assumption that Venice was a fabulously wealthy maritime power.

The temporal dislocation was a big fault. As often with Miller, small faults abounded too. Portia and Nerissa left for Venice in a carriage. Upon returning they were to be seen toiling (or rather Nerissa was to be seen toiling while Portia, free of luggage, walked – a nice touch) for miles through the

75

grounds of their house. So what happened to the carriage? Perhaps the horse drowned.

With all that, though, the production had Mind. This is the quality one is grateful for to Miller: it's the chief reason why his productions, when they reach television, are less of a piece but hold more of interest than the common output of classic drama. To show, in their first scene together, Antonio and Bassanio acting *friendly* to Shylock was to bring out the tension of the gentile/Jewish relationship far better than with the normal postures of ill-concealed hostility. Spitting on the gaberdine had been translated to a more gentlemanly but still intolerant ambience, where Shylock was welcome in the boardrooms but somehow never got elected to the clubs.

A lot more such transforming thought, and the evening might have been saved. But alas, the supply was thin, leaving Olivier to create a whole world on his own. It had been said of the stage production that he took refuge in impersonating the George Arliss portrayal of Disraeli, but any fan of Walt Disney comics could turn on the set and see at a glance that he had modelled his appearance on Scrooge McDuck.

Whatever Olivier had done to his front teeth left his long top lip curving downwards in a fulsome volute on each side, producing a ducky look to go with his quacky sound, since for reasons unknown he had chosen to use a speeded-up version of his Duke of Wellington voice. When he put a top-hat on over all this, the results were Disney's canard zillionaire to the life, and one couldn't refrain from imagining him diving around in Money Barn No. 64 while bulldozers stacked dollars and the Beagle Boys burrowed through the wall. In a way he's still too young for the role: his energy gave the lens a gamma-burn in the close-ups, and at one point of anger he broke into the hyena-walk of Hamlet heading for the platform or Richard looking for a horse.

Crippled, the evening slogged bravely on. The Prince of Morocco did a coon turn: 'As much as ah deserb! Wah, dat's de lady.' Two terrible sopranos sang to Bassanio. A good

giggle, but why would Portia have them in the house? There
are no indications in the text that she is meant to be tasteless
—only that she is meant to be hard, snobbish and dull.
There is nothing to be done with Portia, a point upon which
Joan Plowright lavished abundant proof.

17 February, 1974

Hermie

OVER the past five years television has been instru-
mental in convincing humanity that unless it has a
vasectomy and learns to recycle its non-biodegradable
flotsam, it will be smothered by a rising tide of empty detergent
containers on or about April 1979. This impression being by
now well ground in, the new fashion is to set about reversing it.

Broadly, the shift is from the gloomwatch mood of
Professor Ehrlich back to the good old dependable zest and
bounce of Bucky Fuller, who cheerily regards energy crises
as the merest blockages in Spaceship Earth's fuel-lines, easily
cleared by the whirling Dyno-rod of the human intellect.

Embodying this change of emphasis on a massive scale is
fat-man futurologist Herman Kahn, hugely in evidence this
week in a Horizon called *The Future Goes Boom!* (BBC2).
Roly-poly Herman first reached fame as a Thinker about the
Unthinkable, dreaming up Scenarios for the conduct of
nuclear war. In the Pentagon his message went down like a
50-megaton bomb, since thinking about the unthinkable was
an indispensable preliminary requirement to financing it.
Inspired by this success to an ever more panoramic view of
the future, Herman went into business as a panoptic clair-
voyant. Gradually the negative aspects (e.g., the prospect of
total devastation) got played down. More and more it
turned out that the years ahead were viable, even rosy. He
saw the future, and it worked.

Like Enoch Powell, Kahn has the knack of convincing people who in the ordinary way know nothing about what constitutes intellectual distinction that he is intellectually distinguished. His purported I.Q. of 200 is bandied about like Powell's Greek. Bernard Levin—than whom, usually, no man rates higher for acerbity and gorm—has been seen arriving at Kahn's feet by helicopter and nodding thoughtfully at the very kind of *ex cathedra* fol-de-rol which in the normal course of events he would greet with a penetrating raspberry. And if Kahn fooled Levin, he made a turkey of Brian Gibson, who in producing this programme put a glaring dent in his track-record as a documentary whizz-kid. Renowned for his programmes on Venice and Charing Cross Hospital, Gibson should have been smart enough to lay on some opposition that would pin Kahn down. As it was, the fat man was left free to toddle.

The really fascinating thing about Kahn's predictions is their predictability. With the aid of his colleagues in the Hudson Institute—an outfit which hires itself out on a global basis as an ecosystematic Haruspex—Kahn is able to focus a divining eye on a country rich in natural resources and predict that it will get rich. Similarly he is able to glance at the figures for a country poor in natural resources and predict that it will get poor. But genius is nothing if not flexible, and the Institute is proud of having discovered, all of 10 years ago, that Japan would become a leading world Power. The true marvel, of course, would have been to discover anybody who ever thought anything else, but you can't expect miracles. Kahn's boys don't claim to be infallible: merely prescient.

Kahn speaks a personal language featuring units of time and distance otherwise unknown to science. In particular, the auto-extruding temporal unit 'fivetenfifteentwennytwenny-fiveyearsfromnow' crops up often enough to be worthy of a name. On the analogy of the Fermi (the diameter of an electron) I propose it should be called the Hermie. Kahn's

First Law of Ecodynamics can then be simply stated. In the space of one Hermie, anything that is happening now will still be happening only more so, unless something stops it. (The Second Law states that the fee for being told the First Law will be very large.)

Apart from their predictability, Kahn's predictions are also notable for their vulgarity, as in his notion that future wealth will allow everybody two cars and a helicopter each, plus access to free-fall sex. A sociologist from the University of Kent was allowed just enough screen time to point out that Kahn's preachings constituted an ideology, but not enough to outline which ideology it was. The producer's hope, I suppose, was that Kahn would condemn himself out of his own mouth. The hope was pious, placing too much trust in the efficacy of self-revelation. A quick salvo of incisively expressed disbelief would have done wonders.

10 March, 1974

Fortune is a woman

SCREEN awards mean little, but it didn't hurt for *Whatever Happened to the Likely Lads?* (BBC1) to be singled out in the recent honours list, since the show has been a very present help in times of trouble.

Terry had a line to fit the week. 'You've got your whole lives ahead of you,' he told Bob, currently deserted by the steely Thelma. 'You're just at the dawn of your disasters.' Here was a comic motto peculiarly appropriate to the tragedy unfolded by *Children in Crossfire* (BBC1), an unpretentious and paralysing documentary about what is happening to young minds growing up in the hot-spots of Northern Ireland. One glimpse of its nightmare footage would have made Pangloss into a Manichee – it radiated evil like a handful of weapons-grade plutonium.

Writer-producer Michael Blakstad's approach was more impressionistic than statistical. I would have liked to hear more figures for once, but meanwhile what documentation there was was plenty to be going on with. The kids' school exercise books were more than enough to convince you that their brains were in turmoil. Not only did doodles of tanks and planes abound – nothing unusual to my generation in that – but every drawing of life at home was complete with soldiers bursting through the front door. Toy guns are the first things the children build. They play in patrols instead of gangs, prodding suspects up against the wall for a quick spreadeagle and frisk. That they copy the intrusive squaddies rather than the indigenous gunmen is apparently no mystery – psychologists call it Identifying with the Aggressor. Naming the phenomenon, however, is clearly no solution to the problem.

Hyperactive by day, disturbed children scream in the night. Lulling drugs are prescribed: tots shamble eerily about, tranked. Farther up the age-range, there are pre-adolescents who can't wait to get into the real fighting. A Protestant volunteer called Billy was interviewed. Glowing with pride from a brilliant career of beating up his schoolteachers, he was mad keen for any duty the U.D.A. might require of him. Catholic equivalents were manifestly on hand in large numbers, but weren't talking. This was a mercy: one such mutant was amply sufficient to scare the daylights out of you. He probably scares the U.D.A. as well, since in the unlikely event of victory he will be no easier to dismantle than a booby-trap with a trembler fuse.

Like a minced hydra the hatreds renew themselves from generation to generation. In the face of such propensities to murder, it is hard to see how the troops can stay, and harder still to see how they can go. Possibly we are faced with a Thousand Years War, only half over. Analyses err, it seems to me, which see the disaster in Ireland as conforming to the ordinary pattern of anti-colonialist insurrection. This, surely, is a true Holy War, conducted between forces which show no discernible differences to the outside eye, and the real parallels are close to home, in European history — particularly, I think, in the history of the Low Countries. In that parallel lies the magnitude of the catastrophe and the one ray of hope. Those wars were clearly all set to last for ever, but there came a day when even they burned themselves out. Children stopped drawing the Duke of Alva and stabbing one another with toy pikes. The agony only *seemed* eternal.

A point worth remembering when contemplating *Napoleon and Love* (Thames). Already a third over but somehow seeming as endless as the Gobi, this series is a turkey of fabulous dimensions, able to trot for hundreds of miles before laying its enormous egg. 'Darling!' cries Thérèse. 'Thérèse!' yelps Josephine. Too good an actress to invest such blague with a single atom of belief, Billie Whitelaw plays Josephine with the effortless desperation of Rubinstein playing 'Chopsticks' — to her infinite credit, she has never been so bad in her life. 'No one but you knows how to tie a cravat!' she trills to Captain Charles, the sweat of embarrassment gleaming in her eyes like glycerine. 'Put that line on my tombstone,' laughs Charles (Tony Anholt, poor bastard) 'and I shall die happy.'

Or was it Murat said that? I can't remember. Anyway, Josephine laughs the Period Laugh, the one that starts with N. 'Nha-ha-ha-ha!' (Variations are 'Nho-ho-ho-ho!' and 'Nhee-hee-hee-hee!'). Charles is dressed as a captain of Fusiliers, or is it a colonel of Cuirassiers? He is frogged, freaked, fluked, furred and feathered. Peter Bowles (a good actor here drowning vertically, as a brave man should) plays Murat, who is dressed as an admiral in the Brigade of Horse, or it could be an air commodore in the Fleet of Foot: he is pleated, prinked, pampered, powdered and plumed. Asked, in one of the show's typical directorial coups, to wheel past camera before delivering a flaccid epigram to some group of revelling young dancers going 'Nha-ha-ha-ha-ha!', Murat looks and sounds like a robot camouflaged with Christmas decorations.

When Murat and Charles, or is it Marmont and Muiron, are on screen together the exposition coils more densely than the smoke of cannon. 'You realise that now General Blanque, liberating and plundering in the South, has decoyed the Austro-Hungarian archdukes away from Milan, the way is free for Bonaparte, in command of, to, after which ... ' But they are interrupted by the silky rustle of a wanton chemise. 'Darling!' 'Thérèse!'

Someone says 'Fortune is a woman.' 'Nho-ho-ho-ho-ho!' The camera does a sexy slow zoom through the candlelight, represented by 10 million kilowatts scorching down from the gantry and lighting up the set whiter than a hospital's bathroom—it's an all-neon Directorate. We dissolve to the transalpine bivouac of the all-conquering Bonaparte, played by Ian Holm with a ratty haircut and one hand inside his tunic, doubtless clutching the fatal contract to which his signature is irrevocably affixed. 'I am a Corsican,' he declares, for the benefit of those in the audience who thought Napoleon was a Mexican. 'We have second sight.' Later on he started telling Josephine something about her stomach. It could be that he wanted to march on it, but I fainted before I could find out.

17 March, 1974

What Katie did

THE mood for the *Eurovision Song Contest* (BBC1) had already been set by *Radio Times*, which gave over its front cover to a sparkling tableau showing the Responsibility of Representing Britain being handed on by veteran Cliff Richard to his awed successor, Olivia Newton-John.

Displaying sixty-four unblemished teeth between them, the two young people looked so blazingly hygienic you wondered if any bacteria could survive in the same room. Could this be Britain's year? I laid in a stock of Cox's pippins from the kitchen and switched on the set.

David Vine was immediately in evidence, giving us a historical run-down on a show which by now involves thirty-two countries and 500 million viewers in a search for Europe's songatheyear. No mean honour, then, that the show this year was being put on in our very own Brighton, where our hostess was the multilingual Katie Boyle. It subsequently emerged that the multilingual Katie was the hit act of the night, translating herself into sexy French with a smile rivalling Olivia's in its dentition. David did his best, though, now and subsequently, to make sure we wouldn't be burdened with actually hearing any of that. Every time Katie broke into the contest's second language, David broke in as well, drowning her with a voice-over which filled us in on the background info relevant to each country. Spain, for example, was 'the land of the package holidays'. It is also the land of institutionalised Fascism, but some concepts are too difficult to handle when you've only got half a minute.

Carita from Finland sang 'Aelae mene pois'. She delivered the song very professionally, in English. We might have been in a concert hall in Brighton. Wait a second—we *were* in a concert hall in Brighton. Anyway, singing the song in English would almost certainly be a break for all those Koreans David kept assuring us were tuned in. Out there on the edge of Europe, Korea probably doesn't boast too many Finnish speakers.

Olivia Newton-John came on. A bit unfair, being on that early: surely the later ones have a better chance. Still, grin and bear it. And what a grin! Those teeth! A skin like Caramel Delight, a gown like a blue nightie—she was the picture of healthy innocence. 'Long LIVE love ... ' How could she lose? The Koreans would be going crazy. 'My goodness she sold that *well*!' cried David, moved. Perhaps he had been afraid that she would forget the words, the song being so much more complicated than the British entries of previous years, and the words being among the most forget-table ever written. But she had not. She had done it. In the phrase once used so memorably by David *à propos* of a famous athlete, she had pulled out the big one.

From Spain came Pedro Calaf, manfully delivering 'Canta y se feliz', a clever number with lots of false endings and no chance whatever. From Norway, billed by David as 'the place where they drink aquavit', came Anne-Karine Strom, trilling a song of which I can recall not a skerrick. From Greece (land of Pythagoras? Praxiteles? Military Govern-ment? David didn't specify) came Marinella, her song blatantly built around three chords, her hopes on sand. The apple-cores piled up. What time would it be in Korea?

But then – sensation. Israel, land of compulsory military service, had unexpectedly come up with, not a singer, not two singers, but a *group!* They were called Poogy. Whereas Olivia Newton-John looks as antiseptic as an intensive care unit in a maternity hospital, Poogy merely looked as sterile as an assembly shop in an optics factory – i.e., compara-tively raffish. Noncomformist in their tank-tops of differing weaves, they riffed their way happily through the kind of number their fathers used to sing on kibbutzes in the lulls between Arab attacks. It would have been nice to know what the words meant. Subtitles could have told us easily, but doubtless the hierarchs are tremulous lest the mass British audience suddenly get the impression it has switched on a Godard movie.

From Yugoslavia, the Korni Group. Suddenly it was raining groups! David said that this lot were terrifically interesting, a bunch of characters, protean, unpredictable, rebellious. Their song, 'The Generation of '42', would be fascinating, especially if they sang it in English instead of Serbo-Croat. They might do either, since there was no way of predicting what they might do. They sang it in Serbo-Croat.

Representing Sweden were Abba, a two-girl and two-man outfit with a song called 'Waterloo'. This one, built on a T-Rex riff and a Supremes phrase, was delivered in a Pikkety Witch style that pointed up the cretinous lyric with ruthless precision. 'Waterloo, Could've escaped if I'd wanted to ... ' The girl with the blue knickerbockers, the silver boots and the clinically interesting lordosis looked like being the darling of the contest. 'Waterloo ... ' There could be no doubt that in real life she was squarer than your mother, but compared to Olivia she was as hip as Grace Slick, and this year, what with Poogy and Korni, hip was in. 'Finally facing my Waterloo'. As the girls clattered off in their ill-matching but providentially chosen clobber, their prospects looked unnervingly good. The hook of their song lasted a long time in the mind, like a kick in the knee. You could practically hear the Koreans singing it. 'Watelroo ... '

Iveen Sheer, singing for Luxembourg, had the best song of the night, 'Bye-Bye I Love You'. Very pretty melody, but too subtle in its impact. No chance. From Belgium, Jacques Hustin, singing the kind of number where you stick your hand out and look at it, like Johnny Mathis or Paul Anka. Time for another apple.

The Netherlands relieved, or anyway modified, the monotony by fielding a team called Mouth and MacNeal. Mouth was billed by the ecstatic David as protean, un-predictable, rebellious. He looked like a fat leftover from a California rock group circa 1969. Cindy and Bert did a big ballad for Germany – cabaret stuff. Piera Martell from Switzerland did another, very fine ballad, 'Mein Ruf nach dir'. 'Would you believe, looking at that face,' David asked romantically, 'that she used to work in a construction company?'

Finally, from Italy, and the only previous winner, the sweet Gigliola Cinguetti sang 'Si'. She was very nervous, and would probably have been hysterical if she had known that she was about to be defeated by the dreary Sweden.

And so it ended, with country after country throwing the bulk of its votes to a pair of silver boots. In Korea, land of peace-talks, they would be going back to work in the rice paddies. A lonely apple-core dropped from my drowsy fingers, forgotten, like a song. Olivia, I'm told, came equal fourth.

14 April, 1974

Noddy gets it on

ON several occasions last week the tube attempted to analyse the complex personality of the creative artist. It came closest to doing this satisfactorily with a *Success Story* (BBC1) about Enid Blyton. The approach was statistical. You needed pencil and paper to get the most out of it.

Miss Blyton, we were informed, wrote 600 books in forty-four years. While the programme's participants went on to discuss the Famous Five, the Secret Seven and the Auto-Erotic Eight, your reporter was busy with a long division sum which yielded, after a certain struggle, the answer 13·64. Call it 13½ books a year. Beat that, Balzac! The screen promptly presented my highly tuned mathematical mind with a further challenge: the 600 books had sold 85 million copies in 128 languages. That made it 141,666·7 copies per title—a figure which would be only an average, since obviously some titles ('Five Go To Pieces') would do better than others ('Seven Synthesise DNA').

Also an average was the figure for copies sold per language: 664,062 precisely. This seemed low, but one could postulate with some confidence that sales in languages like English and Spanish would be massive. It must be the less populous tongues which were dragging the figure down. Try to name twenty-eight languages, and then imagine the tight little groups of people who speak the remaining hundred. Single families in isolated hutments. Cliff-dwelling solitaries reading 'Noddy Pfx Mwrkl Fsg'.

From 1948 to 1952 the Blyton output filled four columns of *Whitaker's Cumulative Book List*. That meant 261 books: more than one a week four years running. Even for her, this figure looked high. Perhaps some previously written books had been included. Her average output over a lifetime was more like one a month: 13·64 when divided by 12 comes out at 1·13. Still astonishing but at least conceivable.

William Feaver, a Blyton-junkie helplessly addicted to the woman's creations, gave a gripping stylistic analysis of a book called (I trust my notes are accurate) *Randiest Girl in the School*. He is so familiar with Miss Blyton's style he can tell where she broke off for lunch. An average of about a book a month (rough figures here – we'll give it to the computer later on) means somewhere around 30 lunch breaks per book, except for the big years 1948–52, when the figure must sink to approximately seven meals per title.

The picture conjured up was of a hunched crone maniacally covering paper while being fed through a hole in her cell door. But testimony was forthcoming to prove that it wasn't like that. Some of the Blyton fans were engagingly keen, and even the detractors seemed to be thriving on their critical task. The women concerned – mothers and/or teachers – were all television naturals. Several of them had the right answer, which is that nobody can predict what will interest kids.

5 May, 1974

Why Viola, thou art updated!

AS an alternative to *Stars on Sunday* for those determined on religious enlightenment, let me recommend *See You Sunday* (BBC1), in which, last week, our old friend the Maharishi got an exemplary grilling about his Transcendental Meditation World Plan, with special reference to the role played in it by money. 'If the Organisation is rich, life will be rich,' the holy person explained. Pressed further on the point, he yelped, 'I don't talk in terms of money ... don't talk to me of *money*.' He wanted to talk about something called 'the individual', and the 'full expression' of its 'creative intelligence'. All obtainable for twenty quid.

There was a Shakespeare play scheduled. Luckily, considering the circumstances, it was a comedy. In fact the BBC2 link-man announced it as 'Shakespeare's evergreen comedy, *Twelfth Night*.' Evergreen, eh? Should be good. 'What country, friends, is this?' 'This is Illyria, lady.' Wait a second, though ... it was Regency England! They'd updated the thing! That meant, as usual, biting your nails for a couple of hours while waiting to see how they handled the scene turning on Malvolio's crossed garters. It's an impossible scene to manage if the updating ensures that nobody, whether Malvolio or anybody else, is wearing any kind of garters—crossed, plaited or helical—at any other time.

It thus having been carefully arranged that the climactic comic scene would go for nothing, it was the merest act of courtesy to ensure that the rest of the play's humour, such as it is, should be extirpated too. Sir Toby Belch was played as a stand-in for Sid James. Malvolio himself was played by Charles Gray, an actor whose perfection of suaveness is funny in itself, but who is therefore quite unable to play

anyone with pretensions — he is already what he is, and can't
be funny trying to become it. It's hard for Malvolio not to
get a laugh when he tries out the smile recommended in
the fake letter, but Gray managed it. To cap all this, the
world had been scoured for a black man who sings as badly
as I do. After a long search, one was discovered, and he was
cast as Feste. The way one's spirits sank when Feste came
capering on is not to be described. Aguecheek, for a mercy,
was passable.

The direction was understandably eager to keep proving
that the show had been shot expensively on location. There
were long tracking shots through colonnades, long static
shots down endless hallways, and a different room for almost
every scene. The whole production would have been
tiresomely incoherent if Shakespeare and Janet Suzman,
hand in hand, had not come running to the rescue. The play's
subtly ambiguous emotional entanglements are just the thing
for Miss Suzman to get involved in, since she, without being
in the slightest degree butch, is none the less a true trans-
sexual actress. She was already established as the only
believable Portia I expect to see, and now she is the only
credible Viola.

Whether Miss Suzman is being a man or a woman, her
deep voice serves her equally well. She has no need to hoot
when playing a man: all she has to do is expunge the
sweetness. When the sweetness floods back in, she is as female
as you could wish. Her face is a classic, making her the kind
of man women call beautiful and the kind of woman men call
handsome. It was easy to sympathise when Olivia fell for her,
even though Olivia's love was declared, Joan Greenwood-
style, from somewhere behind the antrums. It was even
easier to sympathise when she, Viola, fell for Orsino. Not
that there was much of interest about Orsino except for his
habit of using his own stair-well as a drawing-room, but
Miss Suzman's sensuality is an arousingly convincing thing
when she lets it roll. She was in a play all of her own — the one

Shakespeare wrote, in fact. Her speed and delicacy were just what the bard ordered.

Success Story (BBC1) dealt with Tretchikoff, perpetrator of that picture featuring the green Chinese lady. Presented by the droll William Feaver, the show dug up some people to whom this gaudy atrocity was a genuine aesthetic experience. As one who well remembers having admired trash, I found them hard to laugh at. Commendably, the programme didn't find them funny either, but contented itself with recording their enthusiasm. Feaver was well aware that popularity is no simple matter. Tretchikoff himself, however, is right up there beside Samson in the front rank of the Philistines. He wants 'constructive' criticism, he says – the eternal plea of the kitsch-merchant. While waiting for the constructive criticism to appear, he stalks about among his wealth planning new masterpieces.

19 May, 1974

Wisdom of the East

EVEN the most healthy Westerner has only to think back over his own medical history to start uspecting that there ought to be, has to be, another way, or Way: all those powders and needles and gases, all that helpless waiting while the white witch-doctor decides how much he dares tell you. Think what it would be like to run your own organism, instead of it running you! In the face of Yoga no one can afford to feel superior. It was with a proper humility then, that I tuned in to Hugh Burnett's documentary *The Roots of Yoga* (BBC1). Already hushed by the shock of hearing from a reviewer that I was 'over-bright', I was determined from now on to be over-dumb. Un-smart, non-clever, receptive.

'I shrink to the size of an atom and reach out to the moon,' a man said almost immediately. The type of Yoga under examination was Hatha Yoga. The man was sitting in a position that looked fiercely difficult. A friend of mine, who can do the same position, says that there are even harder ones up the line, culminating in a number where your legs double back under your tail and you sit comfortably on your ankles with your feet cupping your behind. The attitudes these chaps could get into were undeniably impressive. For the benefits of getting into them, however, we had to take verbal assurances. Such-and-such a position was good for hookworm and tapeworm.

There was a doctor on hand to say that Hatha Yoga really could deal with arthritis, bronchial asthma, colitis, dysentery and things like that. It seemed more than possible. That someone who could wrap his legs around his head would be an unlikely candidate for arthritis seemed a truism. What about hookworm, though? Perhaps the hookworms can't stand the activity: they pack up and quit.

Water was poured in one nostril and came out the other. A piece of thread, good for adenoids, was introduced into the nose. This was also good for hair and eyes: 'all the organs it is affecting'. It also improved your eyesight. A man swallowed 29 feet of white bandage. 'Yes, but first you have to practise for two days.' This was good for stomach ailments, helped you reduce, and dealt with eighteen different types of skin disease. Since the man had not a blemish on him, he could have said 180, or 1,800 – or rather the man talking on his behalf could have. The man himself was full of cloth.

It was somewhere about here that Hugh Burnett succumbed to a mild panic – induced, I think, by the deadly Eastern combination of visual miracle and verbal tat. When his guide assured him that after the appropriate training the adept would soon be 'sucking the water through the rectum', Burnett, instead of saying, 'Show us, show us,' said 'How? *How*?' Apparently the stomach makes a vacuum and the liquid rushes in through the sphincter to fill the gap. I have no doubt that this happens, but it would have been nice to see a beaker of water marked Before and After held by somebody – Burnett would have been the ideal candidate – who had actually been there when the man sat on it. And the same goes double for the bloke who can suck air through the penis. Not only air, but milk, honey and mercury. 'Mercury!' shouted Burnett, 'why *mercury*? Isn't that dangerous?' 'No,' came the all-wise answer, 'it is not dangerous.'

A man bent a steel bar with his eyelid, but I was still thinking about the mercury. I stopped thinking about it when a much older man smashed a milk bottle and lay down in the pieces while they put a heavy roller over him. There was a fulsome crunching as the small pieces of glass became even smaller pieces. The man rose to his feet long enough to brush a few slivers from his unmarked skin and win a tug-of-war with an elephant. Then he lay down again and they drove a Mercedes truck over him.

Plainly this skill would come in handy any time you fell asleep on a broken milk-bottle in the middle of an autobahn. Apart from that, its only function can be to convince the sceptical that Hatha Yoga gives you power over the body. No arguments, although I would like to know if there is a limit to how much the old man can stand. Suppose you wheel away the Mercedes and bring on, say, a Volvo Thermo-King juggernaut: would he still be lying there, or would he go off and meditate?

The programme wound up by visiting an *ashram* with 120 inmates, half of them Westerners. The *ashram* was meditationsville, and whenever Westerners meditate you have to wear a snorkel, else the rhetoric will drown you. One girl adores her Baba Yogi so much she just likes to stand near him, 'to feel his vibrations. Which, as he is a Perfect Master, are very pure.'

Here was the universe being solved in personal terms, with the Americans being the most self-obsessed of all. 'He knows *everything* ... and yet he has retained his physical form out of pure compassion, because he wants to help us.' The girl's face was lit up like a torch. But it was another girl who took the biscuit.

'My meditations are so intense ... I start doing really *strange things* ... it used to hurt me when I meditated ... it cleansed me, completely cleaned me out ... I can't get enough of my meditations ... because my meditations have taken over my life ... I feel his vibrations coming into me ... it makes me feel love.'

9 June, 1974

Hi! I'm Liza

BAD Sight and Bad Sound of the Week were twin titles both won by *Love from A to Z* (BBC1), a river of drivel featuring Liza Minnelli and Charles Aznavour. Right up there beside the Tom Jones specials in the Bummer Stakes, this grotesque spectacular was fascinating for several reasons, none of them pleasant.

To begin with (and to go on with and end with, since the phenomenon was continuous), there was the matter of how Charles had contrived to get himself billed above the normally omni-dominant Liza. Not only was his name foremost in the opening titles, but the between-song lectures, instead of being delivered by Charles on the subject of Liza's talent, were mainly delivered by Liza on the subject of Charles's genius. 'Hi!' Liza would yell intimately, her features suffused by that racking spasm of narcissistic coyness which she fondly imagines looks like a blush, 'I'm Liza.' (Such a coup is supposed to stun you with its humility, but in the event it is difficult to choke back the urge to belch.) She would then impart a couple of hundred words of material—supplied by someone going under the name of Donald Ross—on the topic of Charles Aznavour, with particular reference to his creativity, magnanimity and vision.

This would be followed by a lengthy and devastating assault on 'My Funny Valentine' by Charles himself, in which the song's subtlety would be translated into the standard emotional intensity of the French cabaret ballad, leaving the viewer plenty of opportunity to note how the tortured singer's eyebrows had been wrinkled by hard times, lost loves and the decline of the franc. Or else, even worse, Liza in person would pay a tribute to Lorenz Hart by singing 'My Romance' as if her task were to put significance into the lyric instead of getting it out. 'You know,' she announced at one point, and I had a sinking sensation that I did, and didn't agree, 'the most that you can ever hope for an entertainer is to *touch* people.'

Liza, who can't even walk up a flight of stairs sincerely (a flight of stairs was wheeled on for the specific purpose of allowing her to prove this), is more touching than she knows. She began her career with a preposterous amount of talent, the shreds of which she still retains, but like her mother she doesn't know how to do anything small, and, like almost every other young success, she has embraced the standards of excellence proposed by Showbiz, which will agree to love you only if your heart is in the right place—where your brain should be.

Liza can't settle for being admired for her artistry. She wants to be loved for herself. Charles, to do him the credit he's got coming as the composer of the odd passable song in the relentlessly up-and-down-the-scale French tradition, is less innocent. In fact he's so worn by experience he's got bags under his head. He knows the importance of at least feigning to find his material more interesting than his own wonderful personality—a key trick for prolonged survival, which Liza will have to learn, or go to the wall. The show was recorded

94

at the Rainbow. It was pretty nearly as bad as anything I have seen in my life, and deepened the mystery of why it is that it is always the BBC, and not ITV, which brings us these orgies of self-promotion by dud stars: package deals which consist of nothing but a wrap-up.

14 July, 1974

Exit Tricky Dick

WITH a measure of dignity but no more candour than usual, Nixon cashed in his dwindled pile of chips. An occasion of some stature, however twisted. It can't be said that television, on this side of the Atlantic at any rate, rose to it.

On the evening of the fateful Thursday, the BBC at 9 o'clock and ITN at 10 o'clock were equally confident that Nixon was about to take the long fall. Obviously each channel's Washington bureau had been doing sterling work: the compilations were pertinent, the pieces to camera cogent. Between the end of *News at Ten* (ITN) and the beginning of what promised to be an historic edition of *Midweek* (BBC1), there was sufficient time to ponder the gravity of the moment. An unprincipled man who had never been fit for his high office was about to be forced from it by due process of law – an event confounding to all sceptics, with the notable exception, perhaps, of the Founding Fathers. In the two and half hours of transmission leading up to Nixon's speech at 2 a.m., the tube would have a chance to excel itself. Like Keats dressing to write a poem, your reporter had a bath and a shave, wrapped himself in a luxurious towelling robe and settled down to take notes.

Alastair Burnet came on and immediately set about conveying a powerful air of relaxation. Condescension

95

permeated his every utterance, as if what we were about to see was a mere formality, the acting out for the masses of a story which had long been known to such cognoscenti as himself. Introducing a satellite link-up, he looked on with weary eyes as the pictures degenerated into a shemozzle. NBC came through on vision and CBS came through on sound. Then neither came through on anything. Alastair celebrated by dropping his phone. A jest and a smile might have helped, but he reserves those for inappropriate moments. Finally we got CBS on both sound and vision. It was meant to be NBC, but who cared? The American telly-men were vibrant with life, well aware that they were living in stirring times. Nixon's staff had been loading household gear into cars. The man himself had been cleaning out his desk. It was going to happen!

If only we could have stayed plugged in to the American networks, everything would have been hunky-dory. But for some reason we were plugged out – perhaps because of costs. So it was all down to our link-men in Washington and London, aided by the standard time-killing compilations on Nixon's career and the blazingly revealing videotape reminders of just how composed and forceful Nixon can look when he is lying his head off. Robert McNeil in Washington was stuck with a pair of unexciting panel members: Hugh Sidey, a portentous but sleep-inducing staffer from *Time*, and Vic Gold, billed as a 'former Agnew aide'. (At least he was used to this kind of thing.) These two weren't going to say anything penetrating about the personality and attainments of the departing giant. Nor was Stephen Hess, who added himself to the team and lengthily revealed that his blandness as Nixon's biographer had in no wise diminished. McNeil asked in vain whether Nixon had a flaw. Sidey said he had, and that it was a disinclination to trust the American people. Gold and Hess said similarly unremarkable things either then or later; it is impossible to remember. Harry Truman said that Nixon couldn't tell right from wrong, but that was years ago: he wasn't around to say it now. You longed for a single cutting phrase.

Back on the home patch, the undynamic Alastair was abetted by Julian Pettifer, who did his best to look keen about interrogating a studio panel only marginally more gripping than the lot in Washington. William Shawcross of the *Sunday Times* seemed quite bright, but there was a man from the *New York Times* who kept saying that Ford would succeed Nixon and therefore cease to be Vice-President and that there used to be a war in Vietnam. Pettifer got impatient: he was probably wondering what Walter Cronkite was saying. So was I. Alastair cued in a rerun of Nixon's odyssey, informing us gratuitously and with small evidence that this had been 'in some ways a more distinguished career than the twists and the turns of the past year and a half have suggested'. He promised us 'a little look' at it. His tones were those of a solicitous father called in by his children to officiate at the funeral of a hamster. Meanwhile the commercial channel was showing *McCloud*.

As we came close to the big moment, the BBC's Washington studio went ape. The ineffable Rabbi Korff, who believes in Nixon with a love that passes understanding, was more or less accusing his hero of trying to frame himself. Galvanised at long last, Vic Gold began shouting at the Rabbi with such violence that the picture went off the air. It was back to Alastair. Time to punch the button. ITN's screen was full of Cronkite, what a relief. The last few minutes before Nixon appeared were thereby invested with some substance.

Nixon has come a long way as a talking head, and never did a smoother gig than his last as President. 'I have always preferred to carry through to the finish, whatever the personal agony involved.' He meant that he had always preferred to cling on to power, whatever the agony involved for other people – but at least the lie was told in ringing tones. I had expected him to look like a cake in the rain, but the impeachment sweat was gone from his top lip and his jaw-line was free from crumples. 'I have always tried to do what was best for the nation.' He was a constitutional disaster for the nation – or would have been, if the Supreme Court hadn't fulfilled its function. Semantically, the whole speech was rubbish. As a performance, though, it merited what respect the viewer could summon.

11 August, 1974

Hot lolly

A NATURE programme entitled *We Call Them Killers* (BBC2) had killer whales. A man played the flute to them. Until they move they look oddly like fibreglass models of themselves. The same applies to the *Osmonds* (BBC1), who were with us every night of the week. Nothing – certainly not the BBC – threatens *them*. The last time I cast aspersions on the Holy Family in this column, letters and petitions arrived by the lorryload from weenies and micro-boppers beside themselves with rage. I got a Snide Reporter of the Year scroll with 200 signatures on it, some of them in cat's blood. One little girl said that she hoped my finger would get inphected and drop off. The tots really care all right, and are ready to forgive the Osmonds their hideous cleanliness in the same way my lot used to forgive Little Richard the foam that dripped from his teeth when he sang 'Tutti Frutti'. I can't help feeling we got better value for our money, but no one stops the wheel.

The Osmonds are capable of some sweet harmonising and guitar-picking offstage, but onstage their act is utter corn – laborious mimes to playback, sub-Motown choreography and mirthless humour. Merrill looks like Philip Jenkinson and little Jimmy (once again the Bad Sight of the Week) must appeal only to children so young they can't cut up their own food. The star, of course, is Donny. He is a cow-eyed, fine-boned lad of the type you see languishing angelically in a Botticelli *tondo*. His acreage of gum is a testimonial to the stimulating properties of the electric toothbrush. His line of patter is based on the sound principle that any reference to the opposite sex, however oblique, will cause its younger representatives to attain orgasm. 'We're having a fantastic time here in Britain. There are so many *girls*.' (From the peanut gallery, a vast cry of 'Eeegh!') 'I have a confessiona make, you know? Yesterday I was talking to this *girl* ... ' (Yaaagh!)

Interviewed by the dutifully attentive Noel Edmonds, Donny sweats like a hot peach ice lolly. 'There must have been a time', ventures Noel perceptively, 'when you realised you were being singled out.' (Eeyaagh!) 'I love it.' (Aaangh!) 'The fans want to get near to you.' (Wheeoogh!) 'I love it.' (Mwaangh!) 'You don't mind being pulled around?' (BLAAEEGH!) 'I love it.' (PHWEEYAAOOGH!) The toddlers are practically suiciding off the balcony, flailing one another with teething rusks. The young in one another's arms. Those dying generations at their song.

18 August, 1974

Rough justice

AS ALWAYS there was trouble in other countries, but it was a quiet week domestically. The screen crawled with patrolling cops. Statistics show that most television police emanate from America and used to be actors: Ironside (Raymond Burr), Madigan (Richard Widmark), MacMillan (Rock Hudson), Cade (Glenn Ford), what's-his-name in *Streets of San Francisco* (Karl Malden), and now Kojak (Telly Savalas). These, and others so obscure I can't remember their faces, constitute a *pax Americana* of dreams. We are importing an ethic which was already a fantasy in its land of origin. The disturbed viewer is left longing for the home brew. Whatever happened to *Z-Cars*? Where is *Softly Softly*? Bring back Harry the Hawk! I never thought I'd find myself saddled with so square an emotion as pining for the indigenous culture.

But even if the man who makes the pinch comes from outside, the trial still tends to be held here. *Justice* (Yorkshire) has now finished another series. It will be sorely missed in our house. On Friday nights it always overlapped *Ironside* (BBC1) by about half an hour. We never punched the button until *Justice* had ended. Anyway it was refreshing, after seeing Harriet through a difficult court case, to switch over and watch the Chief's team working on a problem which you had to reconstruct while they were unravelling it. This gave the programme an element of unpredictability.

Not that *Ironside* really needs anything beyond its archetypal situations. Fran is no substitute for Eve, whose hairstyles were masterpieces of the metallurgist's art, but Ed's light-hearted interchanges with his lovably gruff boss are still there (some psychopath tried to put Ed in a wheelchair of his own a few weeks ago) and Mark goes on grappling with the eternal problem of wringing a performance out of the two lines of dialogue and five reaction shots he is allotted per episode. (Mark's two lines are usually 'I'll make some coffee' and 'Guess I'd better make some coffee', and the variations of emphasis he can get into them are like something Beethoven turned out for Diabelli. His situation demands comparison with that of another token black – the one in *Mission Impossible* who gets no dialogue at all, just the reaction shots. All *he* can do is pose like a corpse in a photo booth.)

Harriet's excuse for leaving the screen is reprehensible. She has ratted out of the sex war by marrying her doctor. If this means giving up the bar it will be a cruel blow for the feminist cause, not to mention for certain sectors of the James family, by whom she has been applauded devotedly as she runs rings around all those bewigged chauvinists bent on incarcerating her clients. After a hard day of duffing-up opposing counsel and shaking the complacency of fuddy-duddy judges, Harriet would clomp back to her chambers and kick her male clerk around the office. The way this pitiful factotum cringed at the sight of Harriet's crocodile-skin shoe was greeted with a purr of satisfaction from sources close to the present writer.

25 August, 1974

The Hawk walks

ELECTION coverage crammed the videospace on my return – a grim welcome. *Panorama* (BBC1) on Monday night featured a triangular interchange between Michael Foot, Cyril Smith and Jim Prior. When somebody waved a finger at them for a one-minute wind-up, they combined into a soaring ensemble like the trio from the last act of *Rosenkavalier*. 'One of the factors ... I'd just like to say briefly ... I think Mr Foot ... I'd, I'd, I'd just ... what it means ... *All I'm saying* ... I'D JUST LIKE TO SAY BRIEFLY ... WHA-WHA-WHA ... ONE OF THE FACTORS ... ' The tone for the week was set.

ITV news staff pulled their plugs, perhaps to pre-empt the oncoming longueurs; but still there was little rest. Taking desultory notes ('Cyril Smith fills the screen like Federico Fellini metamorphosing into a mountain: his shoulders start above his ears') your reporter sweated out the hours until his beloved *Softly Softly* (BBC1) was cranked up into its rightful, majestic slot in the middle of Wednesday night. Readers with long memories will remember how much I had been missing this seminal show in the dreary months before the hols, when the screen was crawling with American actors pretending to be cops and Evans, Snow, Watt and Harry the Hawk were nowhere to be seen. As some people need to wrap a pair of knickers around their heads, I need to see, every week, Snow stand to attention when Watt comes into a room, and Harry the Hawk opening and closing doors. I must have it.

The episode rolled and Harry opened a door in the very first shot. Evans gave a lift to a pair of teeny scrubbers on their way to a pop concert starring Smiling Slim Slavey and the Slavers. They used expressions like 'the bread, daddy' to emphasise Evans's squareness, their hipness and the programme's up-to-dateness. Cut to the village hall (marked VILLAGE HALL), where preparations for the concert are in progress. The programme's budget dictates that there must be long expository conversations between Smiling Slim and his sweating roadie, explaining why there is only one roadie, and an eventual audience, by my quick reckoning, of 36 extras: 'the boys need the airing, they're still not pulling together sweet enough.' Cut to P.C. Snow, telephoning. Still on the phone, he stands to attention when Watt comes into the room, informing him that 'there's what high believe is called a *gig* in Elverton 'All tonight.'

At the concert, where youthful abandon is represented by a lone scrubber clutching Slim's knee, Slim sings a few numbers and is electrocuted. Evans and Harry the Hawk solve the crime. It was the old caretaker who did it. Unable to stand the noise, he pulled out one of Slim's cables. Unfortunately it was the one that earthed the mike. Another contemporary problem had been tackled by Task Force. (Harry the Hawk can also currently be seen on ITV, rippling his jaw muscles in the Mac Market commercial.)

A deeply satisfying experience, that episode, even if it meant having to miss most of *Worldwide: China Today* (BBC2), on which Frank Gillard called Tibet 'an autonomous part of China' without mentioning, as far as I could tell, that China invaded it first. Another fierce clash was between *Twiggs* (BBC2) and *Father Brown* (ATV). I have always liked Twiggy and was sorry to miss her act. Next week I'll be tuned in, since *Father Brown* is nothing extraordinary. It will rate because of its puzzle plots, but judging from this one episode it will have little of the cranky period charm of *Lord Peter Wimsey*. Instead, evenly lit sets and stock performances. Kenneth More, the only actor I have ever heard utter 'Ha-hah!' to indicate mirth, gets by with a few finger-wagging tricks. He didn't say 'Ha-hah!' this time, but he did say 'Hah!' The crime—some buffer getting stabbed in the back—might have stumped Harry the Hawk, but Watt would have solved it in nothing flat. There was a pretty girl, her French fiancé who turned out to be a marquis, an obstreperous young American secretary, a wastrel brother, an unrequited suitor, a faithful dog and the corpse. The last two contended for the acting honours.

Porridge (BBC1) is closer to life, even though (probably because?) comic. Reassuring a black Scots fellow inmate, Ronnie Barker lists all the famous people who were illegitimate: 'William the Conqueror, Leonardo da Vinci, Lawrence of Arabia, Napper Wainwright ... ' 'Napper Wainwright?' 'He was a screw at Brixton. Mind you, he *was* a bastard.' A rock-solid script, by Clement and La Frenais. Good comic writing depends on a regular supply of real-life speech patterns—the main reason why success tends to interfere with talent, since it separates the writer from his sources.

6 October, 1974

Bob's wonderful machines

MADE urgent by a groovy, doomy jazz soundtrack, the title sequence of the BBC's *Election 74* Thursday-night spectacular flashed multiple visuals of Alastair Burnet, Robin Day and Bob McKenzie. Like the bridge of Starship *Enterprise*, the set crawled with purposeful minions and beeped and blooped with monitors, read-outs and displays. Alastair was Captain Kirk. Bob McKenzie was Mr Spock. David Butler was Chekhov and the lovely Sue Lawley was Lt. Uhura. Mission – to Foretell the Future.

The Harris Poll taken after voting, Alastair announced, indicated a Labour majority of 100-plus. 'Bob McKenzie is already on the Battleground.' Most sensational of all Bob's Wonderful Machines, the Battleground is a titanic toy which only its creator can operate or indeed comprehend. Working the slider, Bob showed which Tory seats might fall if the facts followed predictions. 'As we know well in the studio, however,' said Alastair, 'polls and tipsters can be wrong.' How right he was. 'Polls can say one thing but it's actual results that matter.' Right again.

Bill Miller in Glasgow brandished 'our own little Swing-ometer', and said that if the polls were right, the needle was off the dial. 'We are all waiting for the facts,' warned Alastair. 'Facts which can only come from the returning officers.' The first result would probably come from Guild-ford, where Esther Rantzen was in position. '*One* polling officer', trilled Esther vivaciously, 'couldn't *start* his *car,* and actually had to *hitch* a *lift* with his *ballot* box.' Time to introduce the Electronic Results Computer, coyly entitled Eric – a Machine so fabulously complex that not even Bob was allowed to play with it. 'If Eric is happy ... staggering speed ... and he's very fussy ... within microseconds ... a matter of seconds.' A demo run was set up to show how fast

Eric worked. The groovy, doomy music played while he did his number. Cymbals crashed as he produced his results. Mere mortals were prostrate in worship. The hubris was as thick as halvah; you could have cut it with a knife.

As ever, Desmond Wilcox was in Trafalgar Square, cheesed off at having once again been cast as light relief. Eliciting vox-pops in the rain is a bad trip. He was either beamed back up to the starship or eaten by the natives, since he was never heard from again. 'It's time for us to ask ourselves', said Alastair, 'just why we are here tonight.' A quick review of the past year. Michael Steed was introduced — an expert on Tactical Voting. As it turned out, there was to be no tactical voting, so Michael's presence was a trifle otiose. Would Labour have a mandate? Was its majority illusory? David Butler said the predictions had been over-stated. 'I think we might be making too much of it myself,' Bob corroborated, tapping his nose for 'I think' and moving his hands apart to indicate 'too much'. Bob's News-for-the-Deaf hand-signals are an increasingly important part of his act. Marplan in Keighley said the swing might be as low as 1·4 per cent.

We plugged in to Austria to see what they were saying about our election. 'Der BBC und sein Erich-komputer ... ' At 11 o'clock Robin Day appeared sitting at a technological-looking desk beside a mysterious blonde shrouded in shadow. He was talking to Lords Boothby and Shinwell, aged, collectively, about 169 — 'two of the all-time political greats'. Boothby woofled and Shinwell wheezed. Who would succeed Heath? Boothby said it wouldn't be Whitelaw. Shinwell said it ought to be Carrington, but he was in the Lords. Robin observed that Lord Shinwell seemed uncommonly impressed by peers lately.

Sue reported from 'the Battlefront' in London, flashing a still of Alan Watson, once a valued crewman of the starship and now standing as a Liberal. If Alan succeeded it would apparently indicate fulfilment of the Liberal Party's dreams of a solid block of seats. Since any country which could put up with Alan could presumably put up with an oligarchy, this view was hard to refute. 11.5: Esther says that the Guildford R.O. is putting his *jacket* on. The first result must be imminent. No, not yet. Back to Bob, who unveils his New Improved Mini-Swingometer marked BIG PARTY SWING. This transistorised model of his immortal invention looks like being confined, he now thinks, to a tiny differential of 1 per cent. But here comes a fact at last: back to Esther at Guildford. The Tories hold it. Macro Eric ingests the micro datum. While it is being processed, Robin entertains Lords Wigg, Beaumont and Windlesham, advising them not to worry about Alastair Burnet, who is just a parasite. Much heavy banter is fated to be lavished on the subject of what Robin might have meant by this.

At 11.27 the Tories hold Torbay, and the figures are looking dodgy. Bob warns of 'Differential Floatback'. By midnight Margaret Jackson has beaten Dick Taverne, but the Labour majority is looking as thin as a wafer. Robin and Dick Taverne get in touch through the wonders of electronics. 'Good morning, Dick: I can't hear what you're saying.' 'I can hear you.' '*I* can hear *you*.' 'But now I can't hear you.' 'Dick ... ' 'I can't *hear* you.' Bob says that the opinion polls have once again fouled up, and only his Machines possess the truth. Robin gets in touch with Edward du Cann. 'I can't hear what you're saying, Robin.' 'We're *on the air*.' 'I can't hear you through this thing. Can I take it out of my ear?'

At 12.20 Bob is poised before the Battleground. 'This is the area where the two big parties meet head on,' he grits, evoking Bosworth Field and Stalingrad. 'A total nine-pin situation' – there are hand-signals to illustrate this – is apparently now unlikely. 'The Liberal take-off problem' is indicated by the Take-off Graph, which refuses to take off. The Tory victor in Sutton and Cheam strangely thanks his 'helpers who have worked so unavailingly in these past weeks'. At 1.00 Bob wheels on a new Machine, called The Country as a Whole – a map of Britain with little monoliths standing around on it, representing gains, losses and percentages. This Machine is manifestly incomprehensible and little more is heard of it.

At 1.35 Wilson talks to Michael Charlton and promises a hard slog. David's habit of saying 'Conservative' for 'Labour' and 'Labour' for 'Conservative' is by now worsening, but Bob shows no signs of fatigue. He promotes the Swingometer as the great success of the night, and illustrates the meaning of the word 'precarious' by moving his two index fingers around each other. By 3.00 he confidently predicts 'a 10-seat majority situation', later amplified to 'a coming-and-going relationship very near the 1964 situation'. On ITV, the studio is equally full of terrific toys and flashing lights, but Robert Kee and his team are far too normal to compete with the BBC crew.

The long night wore on. Michael Barratt and Brian Widlake took over the bridge while Kirk and Spock got some quick sack-time. At 7.15 the beautiful Sue interviewed Tony Blackburn, who had voted Liberal 'to break the two-party system'. David, too, was still on the bridge, predicting a Conservative – that is, Labour – majority of not less than three, not more than 11: thank you Marplan and good night Harris. Michael Barratt interviewed Katina, the *Evening Standard*'s astrologer, whose predictions had been the same as Marplan's. Uranus was powerful in Wilson's horoscope, but he must watch out for Hugh Scanlon. The economy would start to recover in January.

Bob McKenzie was back at 9.00, saying that 'the theory of swing' had worked 'astonishingly well'. He talked of 'para-landings'. He fiddled once again with The Country as a Whole. In his indefatigable eye glittered the dream of new Machines.

13 October, 1974

Lord Longford rides again

AFTER two dull episodes, *Monty Python* (BBC2) was suddenly funny again, thereby ameliorating the viewing week no end. The pressure on the now Cleeseless team to be as good as ever has perhaps been a little fierce, but that's showbiz.

Anyway, the laughs came and everybody relaxed, including BBC2's link-man, who cheerily postluded the show with a burst of the very same scripted heartiness which Michael Palin had just finished satirising. 'Well, ha-ha, depressions lift and gloom disperses next week, ha-ha, with another visit from *Monty Python*.' Or perhaps the lads had written the links too, as well as some of the rest of the week's programmes, such as *Face Your Image* (BBC1), starring Lord Longford.

Format-wise, the intention of this wonderfully rewarding show was to confront the great man with people's real opinions of his character. What in fact happened was that his chums lined up to flatter the life out of him, so that the only possible area of revelation consisted in seeing how the self-effacing peer would hold up when stimulated repeatedly by electrodes placed in the central ego.

He came through the ordeal with scarcely a tremor. When told how amusing and interesting he was, he took it in good part. When told that he was not only more amusing and interesting than was generally realised, but also far wiser, he bore his anguish like a man. Auberon Waugh, A. J. Ayer, Father D'Arcy and numerous others wheeled successively before the lens to exude hosannas and deploy palm fronds. No severer test of the subject's fabled humility could have been devised. Shyly he was forced to admit that he probably knew more about penology and a few other subjects than anybody else and that perhaps his outstanding gifts could have been used better in the Cabinet, but beyond that he would not go.

The whole deal would have run like an investiture if it had not been for Richard Ingrams, inky editor of *Private Eye*. Ingrams contended that Lord Longford's prison-visits were confined exclusively to inmates who were famous. He further contended that 'programmes like this are probably not a good thing, because they pander to Lord Longford's great love in life, which is publicity.' Abruptly it became apparent that the possibility of Ingrams perpetrating these enormities had not, as far as Lord Longford was concerned, been in the script. Lord Longford, it emerged, had agreed that Ingrams should be on the programme, but that he should be allowed to say these things was a bit much. 'He's been to my house!' piped the wounded noble. But by then it was apparent that all the others had been to his house, too. *Face Your Image* was consequently a bit of a misnomer. *Brush Up Your Self-Esteem* would have been closer to the mark.

Reflecting, not for the first time, that Lord Longford's struggle to attain humility would be somewhat eased by a self-appraisal which faced the fact that he is one of the most conceited men alive, your reporter fell to musing on the conundrum of why the Pakenham dynasty, a family tree of proportions both stately and discreet, should be lit up like a pin-ball parlour in this one branch. What is it that drives the good lord and his beautiful daughters to attempt the common touch by going on the tube, where they prove conclusively to the watching millions that they are about as down to earth as the yeti?

Lady Antonia Fraser's portrayal of Mary Queen of Scots lingers in the memory, and only a few weeks ago, in a programme which the election forced me to leave un-remarked, Rachel Billington was to be seen expounding her life-style as a Novelist. 'Every home should have one,' she crooned, pointing at her housekeeper. Bevis Hillier and similar exotica crowded her lawn for cocktails. There was a Bentley to get about in. 'You see,' she breathed, '*my* dream is real.' One wondered if she had ever heard of Marie Antoinette. But she must have done, from her sister.

'Have you forgotten that we have finally persuaded Honoré de Balzac to come to supper?' Most of the dialogue in *Notorious Woman* (BBC2) is like that. George Sand's circle of intellectuals are an uncommonly witless lot: you would hear better things on Rachel Billington's lawn. The production has the deadly enthusiasm of Hollywood jazzing the classics. An aesthetic discussion between Balzac and George turns into a dance. But the series has its attractions, which I will touch on in greater detail when Chopin appears on the scene. Will he spit tomato sauce on the piano keys while composing the 'Preludes' in Majorca? Watch this space. At the moment, George has just agreed to hurdle into the hammock with Prosper Mérimée.

17 November, 1974

Pink predominates

A PASSION for Churches (BBC2) was Sir John Betjeman's 'celebration of the C. of E.'. Produced by Edward Mirzoeff, the man behind Betjeman's masterpiece about Metroland, the show had not quite the heady scope of its predecessor, but was still very good. 'As I look through this rood-screen,' chuffed the peeping Laureate, 'I can see the colours of the altar hangings. Pink predominates.' Shooting and editing was all done with a delicate touch. The sails of yachts floated in green fields, squeezed and blurred by the telephoto. 'Look at that', breathed Betjeman, 'for vastness and height.' The lens zoomed airily into a vault. We saw bee-keeping nuns at an Anglican convent and the annual festival of the Mothers' Union at Norwich Cathedral, with the smooth Bishop presiding. We saw works of art that it would be folly not to preserve for as long as life lasts. But we didn't hear much about what is to be done with the Church as an institution now that so few people believe in it.

Betjeman climbed the stages of a three-decker pulpit and explained how the local society used to arrange itself every Sunday according to rank, with that pew for the squire, that one for the large farmers, those for the cottagers and those back there for the lesser tenantry. That things don't work so neatly nowadays is a matter for some regret, but a few hints at what Betjeman considers to have gone wrong would have helped. The great merit of the Metroland show was that it saw how the district had been destroyed by its own success: it is not just because of neglect that things pass.

15 December, 1974

Chopin snuffs it

IN the final episode of *Notorious Woman* (BBC2) Chopin croaked. It was a merciful release for all of us.

'Dear George. So cruel,' he wheezed on his death-bed, 'So full of love.' But terminal coughing stilled the soliloquy. 'Aaagh! Glaaack! Eeech! BLARF! BLARF! BLARF!' You couldn't help thinking that the poor bastard was well out of it. Left alone to cope with her daughter, Solange, George tried shock tactics in an effort to bring the giddy chit into line. She tried the split-word technique. ('Your extravagance is be. Yond understanding.') This having failed, she tried black-jacking her wayward daughter with a rubber cliché. ('There's a whole wonderful world outside.') No dice.

But in her declining years George still had friends. Here, for instance, came a venerable figure, shuffling up the garden path. 'You're forgiven,' Solange told her, 'as long as you don't stay up all night talking to Flaubert.' This established that the figure was Flaubert. 'You positively revel in being sixty-eight, don't you?' George asked teasingly, thereby establishing that Flaubert was of advanced years. But how to awaken in the minds of the television audience the realisation that this venerable 68-year-old was the leading literary figure of France? 'You're the leading literary figure of France.'

'Did you know that censorship began with Plato?' Flaubert asked. For some strange reason George didn't. She quoted Diogenes in retaliation, but it scarcely met the mood, so she took to her bed – if I understood the plot rightly – and eventually died of shame. I enjoyed this series hugely, for all the wrong reasons, and will miss it.

David Copperfield (BBC1) is as good as everybody says. It's on a bit early for me, so I was tardy in seeking it out. Steerforth's flaw is well conveyed by Anthony Andrews, and Uriah Heep, played by Martin Jarvis, is a miracle of unction: to hear him talk is like stepping on a toad long dead. But Arthur Lowe's Micawber is better than anything. He follows W. C. Fields in certain respects, but is graciously spoken; and his gestures are as delicate as Oliver Hardy's. Not that his performance is eclectic—it is a subtle unity like everything he attempts. He is also at his peak in the current series of *Dad's Army* (BBC1), which shows few signs of flagging inspiration.

Turner was commemorated, or perhaps incinerated, in *The Sun is God* (Thames), which was a good test of the tuning on your colour set, but left Turner himself looking rather sketchy. During a break there was a Shanida commercial which looked like part of the programme: death imitating art. *Inside the News* (BBC1) was a good series until this week, when sociologists were wheeled on to quell the spontaneity by pointing out the obvious. *Panorama* (BBC1) echoed Des Wilson's recent heart-cry in this paper about housing. A landlord collecting £89 a week from five people crammed into one room did not want to be interviewed.

Mary Quant and Alexander Plunket Greene did. They starred in their very own edition of *Lifestyle* (BBC2), whose fatuous title should have been enough to put them off. We saw their 'little bolt-hole up in the Alps', where they flee to get away from things like, well, *Lifestyle*. 'I love this village because it's a *real* village,' confided Mary. 'It's a *working* village. There are no intruders except us.' Us, and the production team making *Lifestyle*. A dynamic character with a dynamic cigarette held at a dynamic angle struggled with the problem of 'creating', to Mary's desires, *two* types of perfume for the *two* different personalities coexisting in the modern woman.

Mary and Plunket were both insistent that work should be enjoyed, but never got around to tackling the problem posed by the millions of people who are well aware of this, but still don't enjoy their work. 'I'd certainly rather be poor and live in England than be filthy rich and live somewhere else,' Plunket explained, forgetting to add that by ordinary standards he *is* filthy rich, *does* live in England and *does* live somewhere else. These people can't possibly be as foolish as they allowed the programme to make them look. *Lifestyle* is galloping cretinism: a plague on it.

22 December, 1974

Mission unspeakable

NO-NO news report of the decade came from ITN, who speculated darkly about whether the Lizard Peninsula would be hit by pieces of the Saturn rocket making its flaming return to Earth. Cub reporter Stephen Matthews was in position at the threatened site. 'People around the Lizard Peninsula don't seem at all worried about being hit by bits of the American rocket.' He turned dramatically to look at the aforementioned geographical feature while the camera zoomed in to show the rocket not hitting it.

In the current series of *Mission Impossible* (BBC1) the Master of Disguise role is played by Leonard Nimoy, alias Mr Spock from *Star Trek*. For Trekkies this is a disturbing duplication, since it becomes difficult to watch the Impossibles in action without being assailed by suspicions that a leading member of that well-drilled team is suffering from atrophy of the ears. Last week the Impossibles were once again in contention against an Eastern European people's republic, called the Eastern European People's Republic.

The plot hardly varies from episode to episode. A disembodied voice briefs the taciturn chief of the Impossibles about the existence – usually in the Eastern European People's Republic – of a missile formula or nerve-gas guidance system stashed away in an armoured vault with a left-handed chromosympathetic ratchet-valve time-lock. The safe is in Secret Police HQ, under the personal protection of the E.E.P.R.'s Security Chief, Vargas. The top Impossible briefs his black, taciturn systems expert and issues him with a left-handed chromosympathetic ratchet-valve time-lock opener.

The Master of Disguise taciturnly adopts a rubber mask which transforms him into Vargas. A tall, handsome Impossible, who is even more taciturn than his team-mates (and who possesses, like James Garner, a propelling-pencil skull), drives the team to the E.E.P.R., which is apparently located somewhere in Los Angeles, since it takes no time at all to get there by road and everyone speaks English when you arrive. A girl Impossible – who has no detectable function, but might possibly be making out with the top man – taciturnly goes along for the ride.

After a fantastically elaborate deception in which the Secret Police end up handing over the plans of the vault and placing themselves under arrest, the systems expert disappears into the air-conditioning duct and gets to work. A great deal of sweat applied to his forehead, and an abundance of music applied to the soundtrack, combine to convince us that the tension is mounting. A succession of reaction shots shows each of the Impossibles grimly checking his watch. Can the left-handed chromosympathetic ratchet-valve time-lock opener do its thing before the real Vargas blasts his way out of the broom-cupboard and rumbles the caper? Click. The nerve-gas guidance system is in black but trustworthy hands. The Impossibles pile taciturnly into their truck and drive back to America, leaving the contented viewer with just one nagging question: *what on earth has gone wrong with Spock's ears?*

Mission Impossible is glop from the schlock-hopper. *Columbo* (Anglia) tries harder—which in my view makes it less interesting, since although I would rather have art than schlock, I would rather have schlock than kitsch. Here again the plot is invariable. A high-toned heavy commits a fantastically elaborate murder, whereupon Columbo drives up in a pile of junk and is almost arrested as a vagrant by the young cop on duty. (That Kojak can dress so well and Columbo so badly on what must basically be the same salary is one of the continuing mysteries of American television.) Gradually the murderer—last week it was Robert Culp—crumples under the pressure of Columbo's scruffy scrutiny. The plot is all denouement, thereby throwing a lot of emphasis on Columbo's character. As often happens, the character element is not as interesting as the programme's creators would have you believe. *Kojak*, for instance, rates as the No. 1 imported fuzz opera mainly because Telly Savalas can make bad slang sound like good slang and good slang sound like lyric poetry. It isn't what he is, so much as the way he talks, that gets you tuning in.

Barlow, currently re-emergent on BBC1, is what he is, alas. Despite the *Radio Times* articles on the alleged miracles of its making, the series is in fact tedious to the last degree.

The complexity of Barlow's character would have to rival that of Dostoevsky's if we were to stay interested while he concerned himself—as he did last week—with washing up, making coffee and listening to the radio. When he sets his jaws against the foe, the foe dutifully turn pale with terror, but it is difficult to believe. Stratford Johns partly disarmed criticism on this point by cramming himself into the same studio with William Hardcastle on *In Vision* (BBC2) and hinting that he might conceivably be sending the role up.

12 January, 1975

The Turkey in Winter

ONE has tried to give *Churchill's People* (BBC1) a chance, on the grounds that cheapo-cheapo telly will soon be the only kind there is, once the new austerity really starts to bite. Limitations will probably be liberating in the long run: Trevor Nunn's *Antony and Cleopatra*, for example, was a trail-blazing production because it suggested lavishness through economy, whereas most attempts at television spectacle suggest economy through lavishness. *Churchill's People*, alas, suggests little beyond an outbreak of insanity at executive level. Somebody on the top floor has gone berserk.

Last week's episode, 'The Saxon's Dusk', starred John Wood as Edward the Confessor. Wood is one of the best, most treasurable actors we possess—a high stylist. Turn an actor like him, when you can find one, loose on good material, when you can find that, and lyricism will ensue. Give him rubbish to act and he will destroy himself like a Bugatti lubricated with hair-oil.

The script being almost entirely exposition, the characters were mainly engaged in telling one another what they knew already. Since Edward was the centre of the action, he was occupied full time not only with telling people what they knew, but with being told what *he* knew in return. A certain air of boredom was therefore legitimate, which Wood amply conveyed. I myself had never heard dialogue like it, but Edward made it clear that he had been hearing it for years.

'He's making Robert of Whatnot Bishop of London, did you know?' 'A Frenchman to be Bishop of London?' 'He's trying to make us a French colony.' 'But if I leave my nephew as my heir ... ' 'Sire, Bishop Beefbroth has come back: the news is good from Rome.' 'Praise be.' 'The French Bishop is to be disepiscopated immediately.' 'That is good, good.' 'On one condition.' 'What condition, pray?' 'News from Dover, Sire!' 'Dover shall pay dear for this!' 'Your uncle Toxic, Queen of the Welsh, proclaims the Bastard heir!' 'This is the last straw. Where do *you* stand, Bostic?' 'Your half-brother Norman the Exhibitionist's son, Cyril ... '

And so on, world without end. Straining to convey information, the writing reveals nothing about the past of the English people, but much about the present state of the English language. 'While we wait here waiting for the Assembly to assemble ... ' one poor sod found himself saying, and straight away his silly hat looked even sillier, since how can an actor go back through time if given lines mired so inextricably in the present? It was The Turkey in Winter. A two-line exchange of dialogue between a pair of shaggy nobles said it all. 'Why do you not give it up?' 'Because I need the money.'

2 February, 1975

Thatcher takes command

'IT'S a team game we're playing, if it's a game. It's not a game. But we're a team.' This remark, delivered by Colin Shepherd, M.P., on *Midweek* (BBC1) the week before last, struck me at the time as an apposite motto for the current period of Tory confusion. Its neatly circular argument generates a runic impenetrability: the maximum semantic chaos with the minimum effort.

I've got witnesses to prove that my money was on the broad all along. In one addled mind at least, Mrs Thatcher was always a serious candidate. Obviously *World in Action* (Granada) thought so too, since they profiled her last Monday night, a whole day before she established wide credibility by running away with the first ballot. Since Mrs Thatcher probably ranks somewhere near the Chilean junta in WIA's scale of affection, it seemed possible that they were examining her as a toxic phenomenon, like nuclear proliferation or the non-biodegradability of Greek colonels. An air of objectivity, however, was strenuously maintained. Perhaps it was assumed that mere exposure would suffice, and that the sprightly lady would stand self-condemned. It wasn't going to be as easy as that, as events later proved.

But even at that stage, the jaundiced professional eye could detect ample evidence that Mrs Thatcher was working on her screen image with a view to improvement. All political figures try this, but usually they take the advice of their media experts – men disqualified simply by the fact of being available, since nobody of ability would take such a lick-spittle appointment.

It was an expert who told Harold Wilson that he should smile during his speeches, and another expert who told Heath to take his coat off and relax. The respective results were of a corpse standing up and of a corpse sitting down. In America at this very moment it is an expert who is busily convincing President Ford that his speeches will gain resonance if he illustrates them with diagrams drawn in the air. Mrs Thatcher, as far as I can tell, has declined such help, and set about smoothing up her impact all by herself.

Visually she has few problems. The viewer, according to his prejudices, might or might not go for her pearls and twin-sets, and the hairstyles are sheer technology. But the camera loves the face and the face is learning to love the camera back. She is rapidly becoming an adept at helping a film crew to stage a fake candid. While her excited daughter unleashes a hooray bellow in the background and her husband, Mr Mystery, vaults out of the window or barricades himself into the bathroom, the star turn is to be seen reading the newspapers with perfect casualness, right in focus.

The hang-up has always been the voice. Not the timbre so much as, well, the *tone* – the condescending explanatory whine which treats the squirming interlocutor as an eight-year-old child with personality deficiencies. It has been fascinating, recently, to watch her striving to eliminate this. BBC2 *News Extra* on Tuesday night rolled a clip from May 1973 demonstrating the Thatcher sneer at full pitch. (She was saying that she wouldn't *dream* of seeking the leadership.) She sounded like a cat sliding down a blackboard.

In real life, Mrs Thatcher either believes that everybody can help himself without anybody getting hurt, which means she is unhinged; or else believes that everybody who can help himself ought to do so no matter who gets hurt, which means she is a villain; a sinister prospect either way. On the tube, though, she comes over as a deep thinker: errors of judgment like the food-hoarding goof will probably disappear with experience, and are by no means as damaging as the blunders the men perpetrate in quest of screen warmth. ('You know me, Robin, I'm a pretty human sort of chap,' I caught William Whitelaw saying a couple of months ago.)

She's cold, hard, quick and superior, and smart enough to know that those qualities could work for her instead of against. 'Like any winner's dressing room after the big fight, the champagne flowed,' said *News at Ten*, its grammar limp with admiration.

In *Taste for Adventure* (BBC1) a man of incredible strength, bravery and stupidity called Sylvain Saudan skied down the Eiger. 'My head hurt,' he declared Pythonically. In *Inside Story* (BBC2) a cow called Celia was impregnated by a jaded Lothario of a bull called Cliftonmill Olympus II. Cliff produced 5,000 million sperm at a stroke, but never got the girl. The stuff was deep-frozen and transported to the site in a white VW driven by Mr Ray Cod, who donned elbow-length gloves and socked it to Celia with minimal foreplay. Meanwhile Cliff was presumably reading *Penthouse* and preparing himself for further triumphs. Brief encounter.

9 February, 1975

The higher trash

ITS fourth *angst*-ridden episode having been duly trans-mitted to the nation, the Bergman blockbuster *Six Scenes From a Marriage* (BBC2) stands nakedly revealed as the Higher Trash. After more than fifteen years of joyless cohabitation, Ingmar and I are through.

Instead of being equipped with subtitles, a device presumably eschewed as being too off-putting for the hordes of proletarians the Beeb hoped to snare with Bergman's Scandinavian magic, the series has been dubbed, in a fashion so comprehensively disastrous that the reeling viewer suspects the television set of having developed a split personality. Has the tuning mechanism ruptured a rheostat and started picking up an old Lana Turner movie playing on the commercial channel? Certainly no such voices, in this day and age, can be heard anywhere else than in the cocktail lounge of the daily Pan-Am jumbo from Heathrow to Boston as it trails its lumbering shadow across the stratocumulus over mid-Atlantic. Marianne sounds like a well-stoned fashion correspondent blowing bubbles through a dry martini. Johan sounds like the bloke who bought it for her. Separate, they're amazing. Together they're incredible.

The voices violate the dialogue, but since the dialogue is a corpse the crime is necrophilia rather than rape. I imagine, however, that Bergman's heftily deployed sentiments evinced a hint more snap in the original Swedish. The English translation (which for those with a taste for calcified prose can be obtained in a Calder and Boyars paperback at £1·95) is muesli without milk. A single mouthful would be quite sufficient to choke any actor in the world. Guess what Marianne said to Johan in Episode Two, when they were driving along together in the morning? 'What fun it is driving along together in the morning!' And the word 'for' is consistently employed in place of 'because' — a usage hitherto confined to formal poetry and *Daily Express* editorials.

Nobody has ever talked the way these two talk in the whole of English history. The translation is the merest transliteration, which it would have been a matter of elementary competence — requiring about two days of an averagely endowed writer's time — to work up into a speakable text. You don't have to be able to speak Swedish to change 'What fun it is' into something an actress can *say*. All you have to be able to do is speak English.

That the chat clouds the issue, however, should not be allowed to obscure the fact that the issue is dead. The real trouble with the alliance between Marianne and Johan — a trouble which Bergman hasn't begun to examine, being too busy with focusing his pitiless analytical glance — is that they could have no possible reason for being interested in each other in the first place. Liv Ullmann is hardly the earth-mother she is cracked up to be (a few weeks ago in this very newspaper A. Alvarez was to be seen promoting her as a combination of Eleanora Duse, Sieglinde in *Die Walküre*, and Edwige Feuillère), but the awkward truth that she fades on the mind's eye almost as fast as Monica Vitti or Jeanne Moreau doesn't make her entirely weightless: she has more than enough substance to give the diaphanous role she is playing the pulse of real blood. How, though, did Marianne ever seen anything in Johan? And Johan being Johan, how could he have seen anything in her, or anyone?

Johan, functionary of something called a Psychotechnical Institute and failed poet (striving devoutly to distance his own personal experience, Bergman can get only as far as foisting it on a *failed* artist: a non-artist is beyond his powers) finds after years of keeping up appearances with Marianne that his passion for another girl commands him away. So he lets Marianne in for a burst of the bitter truth. 'I'm trying to be as honest as I can – but by God it's not easy.'

What made this scene (the core of Episode Three) unintentionally laughable was Bergman's innocent failure to realise that Johan's sudden cruelty, far from revealing him as a passionate rebel, merely branded him as a perennial zombie.

It is difficult to over-emphasise sex, but very easy to over-isolate it, and Bergman's whole effect is of a puritanical hedonism in which sex includes all possible means of contact instead of being the most important of several. That his characters do not amuse each other is not surprising, since Bergman – despite *Smiles of a Summer Night* and his early grounding in comedy – has a sense of humour considerably inferior to that of F. R. Leavis. But they have nothing else to offer each other either.

In this context, it is natural that sexual gratification should be thought to equal happiness and that happiness should be sought as an end – a monomaniacal defiance of the axiom that happiness is not a worthwhile aim in life, and can exist only as a by-product of absorption. And Bergman's continuing problem is that he is not quite enough of an artist to imagine what people who are not artists could possibly be involved *with*. 'What will I say to the children?' wails Marianne as Johan stomps out. 'Say what you like,' growls Johan, and Bergman honestly believes that he is showing us the interplay of real emotions, instead of putting on a carbolic soap opera. 'If all the people who live together were in love,' says Baptiste in *Les Enfants du Paradis*, 'the earth would shine like the sun.' Nobody is ever going to call Jacques Prévert, who wrote that film, a fearless investigator of marriage – yet compare the shattered pleadings of Maria Casarès with anything that Bergman can provide for Liv Ullmann, and ask yourself which is the explorer, the romantic or the realist.

2 March, 1975

Killer ants

THE viewing week began with the *Cup Final* dominating both the main channels: a dreary occurrence over which we need not waste words, except to say that the supporters were a lot more inventive than the teams. The Fulham banner BUSBY BREAKS BUBBLES was crushingly trumped by West Ham's BILLY BITES YOUR BUM. More enigmatic was TOMMY TRINDER SMELLS GREAT.

On ITV Brian Moore, in lightweight threads of whispering lilac, fronted a brand-new panel of experts – Alan Ball, Kevin Keegan and Malcolm Macdonald, all opinionating flat out in an effort to solidify their new positions. Jimmy Hill's crew on BBC1 were cooler hands: Bobby Charlton, Bob Wilson and the Godfather, Don Revie. Revie liked the way the Fulham squad were all dressed in the same suits and ties. He thought they were 'a credit to the profession'. The Hammers, by implication, weren't. Guess who won.

All this constituted a Mickey Finn of some magnitude, and I woke up somewhere in the middle of BBC1's Saturday Night Movie, *The Naked Jungle*, a film I have been seeing all my life. I saw it when it came out in 1954 and I have seen it in half a dozen different countries since. I have been on a crippled ship in the middle of the Indian Ocean with nothing to watch except *The Naked Jungle*. I once spent a night at a small hotel in a Dutch pine forest and when I turned on the TV it was showing *The Naked Jungle*.

Making an early appearance as the District Commissioner in this superb film was a younger, slimmer William Conrad, more recently known to us as *Cannon* (BBC1). Whereas nowadays Conrad is very fat indeed, in those days he was simply very fat. Of all the film's great lines of dialogue, the greatest is spoken by Conrad. When Charlton Heston announces his intention of fighting the killer ants, Conrad grimly warns him, in a French accent, that he is 'up against a monster 20 miles long and two miles wide. Forty square miles of agonising death!'

Between the end-title of *The Naked Jungle* and the opening credits of *Cannon* half an hour later, Conrad put on five stone. It was a mind-blowing effect. From being merely a barrage balloon, suddenly he was the Graf Zeppelin. Goaded by my post-Cup *tristesse* into feeling even more callous than usual, I was disposed to find this funny. And in *Cannon* fatness *is* funny, because the issue is so thoroughly dodged. Cannon is so fat he has to lean backwards or he'll fall over, yet the pretence is kept up that his largeness happens mainly because he's peckish. He's a gourmet, not a guts. You never hear anything about what it's physically and psychologically *like* to be fat—the thigh-chafing, self-loathing reality is left out.

So completely is the nub of the matter fudged that

Cannon is allowed all the attributes of the slimmer sleuths he is supposed to be different from. When he hits the heavies with the edge of his pudgy hand they collapse unconscious, instead of bursting out laughing. Trained assassins toting hunting rifles equipped with telescopic sights are strangely unable to shoot him: compared to Cannon a barn door looks like a lemon pip, yet they blaze away at his toddling form without being able to score so much as an outer.

There is more of the truth about fatness in *The Girls of Slender Means* (BBC2), a promising new three-parter adapted from Muriel Spark's novel. It is 1945. On the May of Teck Club, a glorified boarding house, all kinds of well-bred girl converge. Jane Wright, played by Miriam Margolyes, is the fat kind. This is already a fine performance and bids fair to develop into something marvellous. Without allowing her chummy niceness to slip an inch, Miss Margolyes looks on in repressed anguish as the man she adores swivels his glance towards the Club's svelte siren. The conclusion we must draw is that Jane's chummy niceness is compulsory: people expect it of her. Miss Margolyes has a richly comic talent which was once conspicuously consumed by *At the Eleventh Hour*, a doomed satire show she was the only good thing in. It is to be hoped that she will now become established as a gift to our screen.

Arthur Hopcraft's new play *Wednesday Love* (BBC2) was a subtle effort even for him, and one hesitates to bruise it with a summary, but to put it briefly: two frustrated suburban wives playing truant on a Wednesday afternoon met two broke students in a drinking club. The brash lad got off with the raver and the quiet ones, Chris and Jean, were left with each other. But it was in their lives that things happened. Chris (Simon Rouse) was bright, but Jean (Lois Daine) possessed the emotional education. Was he callow, or just cold? Was she wiser, or just older? In the end she ran away with him, but you guessed he would soon use her up. The play was directed by Michael Apted and had a lot in it. I hope the tapes of Hopcraft's plays are being kept. He can write better about love than almost anyone, giving you the sense that he has been every character he creates, in their frailties as well as in their strengths.

Scenario: The Peace Game (BBC1) was an epic nonsense about a supposed European crisis in 1978, with real-life ex-NATO bigwigs and erstwhile diplomats improvising limp dialogue behind desks. Being concerned with the Future, the show was naturally fronted by James Burke, who said 'What you are about to see is unscripted,' as if that was somehow a guarantee of excitement. In the event, the proceedings crept by like forty square miles of agonising death. 'May I', asked a Dutchman, 'state the position of the Low Countries?' And he did. A boring Frenchman with a joke accent said: 'I'm going to give you the bottom of my thinking.' And he did.

Pierre Salinger played the President of the United States, a role he was bound to enjoy, since it gave him the opportunity of pretending to be his hero, Kennedy. The President was one of 'two men, each of whom', according to Burke, 'could destroy the planet.' Pierre *loved* being one of those. Talking of 'a normalisation situation' and 'the last resort situation if the thing gets down to the point when it's not tolerable any other way', Pierre inadvertently demonstrated that the language of Watergate began at Camelot.

11 May, 1975

What is a television critic?

HAVING declined to appear on *Don't Quote Me* (BBC2), I'm in no position to bitch about its summary treatment of a complicated topic such as the Critics. Perhaps more would have been achieved if the panel had been graced by my wise and eloquent self, but somehow I doubt it. The joint was already jammed with good men and true, tussling devoutly and getting nowhere.

Bryan Magee was chairman. As our chief lay expositor of Karl Popper's philosophy he knows all about the high value to be placed on the activity of criticism, but dutifully stuck to questions instead of answers. The answers came from such as Michael Apted, Anthony Shaffer, Milton Shulman and Derek Malcolm: men of parts all (although Malcolm seems oblivious of the difference between one medium and two media), but scarcely in Popper's league as rigorous intellects. Nevertheless Magee managed to look interested.

There was a good point from Shulman: to the public there is no such thing as the Critics, since the public mostly reads one paper at a time. Apted, in real life a drama director on screens both large and small, looked as if he wished he hadn't come, but got in a subversive dig at television critics. There is no such thing as television criticism, he said: there are only essayists, of whom he reads the most entertaining. This statement contrived to patronise anybody it did not dismiss — a deft tactic.

It was generally agreed by the panel, or at any rate tacitly conceded, that television critics know nothing about the medium they criticise. Thus was confusion confounded. Most television critics know far too much about television: they are tube-struck in the way most drama critics are stage-struck, and capable of every discrimination except the vital one of telling live inspiration from dead. I am not defending ignorance—only saying that knowledge is no cure for lack of critical talent. And unless he likes jokes with no point, critical talent is what Apted appreciates in the essayists he finds entertaining. So he would be better off allowing that there *is* such a thing as television criticism, and then asking himself why it is different from other kinds.

The chief difference is that it can't readily refer to the past. Criticism which does not reflect the medium's ephemerality and multiplicity (which are aspects of each other) is lying. Apted's part of television is only one part and by no means the characteristic part: in fact he would do it in the form of movies if he could. Television is a thousand different things happening behind a window. It is difficult to be sure what a serious critic of such a cataclysm of occurrences would sound like. It's a safe bet, however, that he would not sound solemn.

Take *The Girls of Slender Means* (BBC2) as an example. At the time of writing I have seen two of its three episodes, each of them twice. It is a marvellous achievement on every level. The intelligent layman (which the good critic must never cease to be) can easily see how sensitively the tone of Muriel Spark's novel has been taken over by the adaptor, Ken Taylor, and how the actors are thoroughly at home in their roles. The critic who has managed to pick up some inside knowledge can further see that Moira Armstrong's handling of cameras is outstandingly sensitive to nuance and in certain scenes, such as the ones set in the dining room, a triumph of sustained virtuosity.

But already I have left out the contribution of the producer, who is quite likely to have been the driving force of the whole project. Or it might have been the script-editor. Even for the critic who has spent a good deal of his time working in television, it is difficult to sort out who did what just from looking at the screen. If he started talking about the accumulated achievement of Moira Armstrong he might be cultivating a myth as well as straining the reader's patience. The *auteurs* who emerge from television – Russell, Gold, Loach, Apted – were never really in it, in the sense that a few score gifted, prolific but necessarily not very famous people are in it and of it. So long as television is various there will be room for what these latter people do, just as, so long as the Church was taken for granted, there was room for a Latin Mass. Television is for everybody. It follows that a television critic, at his best, is everybody too – he must enjoy diversity without being eclectic and stay receptive without being gulled.

The Male Menopause (BBC2), a sub-sociological drone-in fronted by Michael Parkinson, was the mental equivalent of navel-fluff. Nasty rumours have been circulating that I sent Parkinson a forgiving letter after he bored his audience by being rude about me on the air. A calumny. As I once explained to Alan Whicker, who wonderingly inquired why I always called him deplorable, one of the effects of television is to make front-men over-mighty. It follows that one of the tasks of television criticism should be to remind them they are mortal.

Here was a diaphanous topic being given substance by standing Michael Parkinson in front of it. The aim was seriousness plus humour, but the seriousness was not serious and the humour was not funny. A man dressed up to look like a doctor gave what was supposed to be the medical consensus on this subject. In fact, a medical consensus on this subject does not exist, and the doctor was an actor called Peter Howell, cast for the role because he used to be in *Emergency – Ward 10*. Actors are rarely in a position to refuse work. Frontmen like Parky are. Hence the flak.

18 May, 1975

Problem children

MIRTH-QUELLING stories of unhappy children dominated the week, moving the average viewer to bless his own luck, while cursing luck itself.

Carol's Story (BBC1) was a Midweek Special filmed by Angela Pope on behalf of the National Children's Home, which is to receive the fee. One trusts it will be princely. Actresses re-created the life of a woman who had been brought up in deprived circumstances, sick for affection, and who was now passing on the same deprivation to her own children. It was a familiar story but sharply told, leaving you with a clear picture of unhappiness breeding itself in geometrical progression. The responsible social worker was doing his admirable best to reverse what looked dispiritingly like a one-way tide.

An 'Inside Story' called *Mini* (BBC2) dealt with an altogether less recognisable case, who superficially was not so depressing, but who in the long run got you down equally thoroughly. Michael, alias 'Mini', is a handsome, clever, inventive eleven-year-old with the enchantingly gravelly screen presence of the 'fifties child star, George Winslow. Running dialectical rings around his earnest interlocuters, he performed for the cameras with the most astonishing ease. He is a natural actor. He is also a firebug, who on two occasions has tried to burn his own house down while his father was asleep upstairs.

At the Aycliffe Assessment Centre, dedicated attempts were made to uncover Mini's motivations. 'Why do you steal fire lighters, or is that a stupid question?' 'No, it's a reasonable question.' It is very easy to sit at home offering gratuitous advice when worried specialists and desperate parents are grappling with a problem apt to burst into flames at any moment, but I couldn't help thinking that Mini was simply too bright for his surroundings. His parents, obviously good folk both, pathetically tried to put God into him, when it should have been plain that he wasn't having any.

And the psychologists (who will read this with scorn) might have at least considered the possibility that Mini, on his own evidence, is more creative than destructive. The theatre is in his blood. A sawn-off Max Reinhardt, he arranged a song-and-dance routine for his sisters. Round-eyed he recounted the overwhelmingness of his pyrogenetic urge when he discovered a fireplace full of crushed-up newspapers, plus a virgin box of matches on the mantelpiece. 'I thought: this is too much temptation. *It's got to happen!*' He's a dazzling kid, the best company you could wish for. Unfortunately if you take your eye off him he'll burn you to the ground. At the end of the programme he was being shipped away, for extended treatment. One way or another we shall be hearing from him again, I hope, or fear.

15 June, 1975

Biggest bitch in Fleet Street

AFTER earning its place by providing food for thought – or anyway instigation for hurling abuse at the screen –with at least every second programme, *Don't Quote Me* (BBC2) ended its maiden series. In the old *Line-Up* days, before Joan Bakewell became very Sanderson, discussion shows of this ilk were thick on the ether, but the moving finger writes, and having writ, splits, and most of the old topic-balancing talk-fests have long since gone wherever it is that clapped-out formats go to die.

Bryan Magee, D.Q.M.'s frontman, is of course *sui generis* and not to be thought of as a typical BBC2 late-night talking head. Magee is a man of first-rate mental powers. Scarcely the ideal choice, then, to referee a verbal tag-wrestling match organised on the venerable *Line-Up* principle of letting four pundits—two from each side of a burning issue—hurl themselves around for a period precisely five minutes shorter than the time required to get anywhere.

But on the other hand, who better qualified? The distinction of his appearance, the polished carpentry of his sentences, the perspicuity of his intellect! Surely here is the man to bring order out of chaos, even when the topic is Women and the Press—as indeed, this time, it was. Present in the studio were Margo Macdonald, Mike Molloy of the *Mirror*, Anna Raeburn and—slow on the draw but tall in the saddle—Jean Rook, who is reputed to earn more money than any woman in Fleet Street, for reasons which escape me. Probably she draws the bulk of her massive screw in danger money, to offset the lacerating cortical damage she must sustain when reading her own prose.

Macdonald was understandably cheesed off at being described by the *Mirror* as 'the blonde bombshell M.P.' who 'hits the House of Commons today'. Molloy pointed out that this particular fatuity had less to do with the perpetuating of a stereotype than with the fact that hundreds of people are involved in getting out a newspaper and some of them are more tardy on the uptake than others. His objection was overridden in a general rush, headed by Macdonald and Raeburn, to agree that the Press still tended to put Woman in her Place, propagating the idea that no career-woman is quite normal unless she is a housewife to boot, and continually focusing on the irrelevant issue of personal appearance.

Rook shared their opinion, but also shared Molloy's opinion, which was that the Press treated men in roughly the same way. Molloy can only have meant—Magee failed to press him on the point—that the newspapers talk as trashily about men as they do about women, a point made overt by Rook, who quickly assured us that she herself wrote the same kind of vivid, fact-filled prose about either sex. Such details were the stuff of journalism, she asserted. But there were limits. 'I'd slit my throat before I'd use certain emotional words,' she announced, apparently unaware that the proposition was scarcely one that could be made by anybody laying claim to a level head. 'They call me the biggest bitch in Fleet Street.' But she was a liberal deep down where it counted.

It became obvious that to Rook being liberal meant keeping up with the new trends. Unusually prone to writing and talking in clichés ('I'm a classic case,' she averred, correctly), she nevertheless commands a sure sense of the proper time to trade in one set of bromides for another. Magee read some of her own prose to her. It bore out the Macdonald–Raeburn case in all respects, but Rook was in no whit abashed. *That* was written in 1971, she protested confidently. *Everybody* thought that *then*.

Margo Macdonald said the most sensible thing of the night, which was that the real problem had less to do with the way the Press treated well-known women than with the way society treated millions of anonymous ones. But nobody mentioned that an ideal of justice can be only partly realised in life, since a great part of life is the result of natural dispensation, and nature has no conception of justice. Even when all other things are equal, certain gifts must still be portioned out unfairly. For example, both Margo Macdonald and Anna Raeburn are very beautiful, a distinction between them and other women which is likely to increase as other distinctions narrow.

Both women are obviously enraged that opinions of their merits should be mixed up with appreciation of their looks. It's an unselfish rage to have, but it ought not to obscure the possibility—which Magee might have asked them to consider, given time—that the freedom for the individual which both favour could in the long run entail misery for the unattractive, who will be deprived even of their dreams.

Women's Lib-wise, television lags some distance behind the Press, and within television itself ITV trails the BBC. Considering the amount of self-congratulation ITN goes in for when comparing itself to fuddy-duddy BBC News, it might be salutary for the dynamic youngsters to contemplate the increasingly obvious fact that whereas Auntie has got Angela Rippon running a whole *News Extra* on her own, *News at Ten* is still sending Angela Lambert to Ascot.

Lord Chalfont interviewed *The Shah of Iran* (BBC1), who spoke mystically about the 'very specific and special relationship between me and my people'. There's nothing like absolute power for facilitating an insight into the people's will. 'I can claim', he claimed, 'to have the pulse of my people in my hand.' The pulse being especially prominent in the throat, this seemed more than likely.

22 June, 1975

Rancid coils

DOGSHIT! The very name is like a bell, to toll me back from thee to my sole self.

In a commentary admirably willing to call a load of crap a load of crap, the gooey substance was several times alluded to by this disyllabic epithet during *The Case Against Dogs* (Thames), an uninspired but in my view unanswerable assault on the British public's insane fancy for the pooch. Dogshit. Why doesn't everybody call it that? What's in a name? A turd by any other name would smell as rank.

Unfortunately most of the relevant officials interviewed on the subject, both here and in Louisiana (where control of the canine pest is taken with exemplary seriousness), were mealy in the mouth, however hot they might be on the trail. On both sides of the Atlantic dogs were referred to as

defecating rather than shitting. Camden Council employs a
lone inspector to walk the pavement on the lookout for
citizens allowing their dogs to foul it. In a sane society he
would command a department called Shitwatch and wield
the powers of Richelieu. As things are, he pounds the beat
in solitary impotence, a dog-dogging Dogberry, with a
jokey notebook and a Hugh Scanlon vocabulary heavily
adorned with admonitory phrases like 'inasmuch as', 'with
a view to', and 'wherefore so deposit'.

Camden's share of London's million dog-owners answer
this good man back with the insolence customary among
those who treat animals like people and people like animals.
In the unlikely event of his making the charge stick (the dog
practically has to poo on his shoe before he can make the
pinch) he can hope to see the offending owner stung for
twenty quid at most. A worthy type, but valueless as an
instrument of terror. If the law gave him the option to
retaliate by entering the malefactor's house and taking a
swift crap in the parlour it would be a different matter.
People would then be more apt to think twice before
encouraging their beloved pet to drop its guts.

There was some pathetic footage of the only two purpose-
built dog-lavatories in London. Needless to say, these
constituted the few remaining square yards of open space in
the entire city which were not thoroughly impregnated with
cloacal slime. Dogshit, it seems, contains indestructible
worm larvae which transmit themselves to one in twenty
children who play in parks. The larvae cause disease in a
significant number of cases, and in a significant number of
those cases the disease expresses itself as damage to the
eyesight. Eyeballs have been cut out of children because
dogs have been allowed to dump their lunch on the grass.
It's my experience that most dog-owners would regard this
as an acceptable risk: they are usually experts at ascribing
to the will of nature the havoc wreaked by their jealously
cherished vermin.

Near my house in Cambridge is one of the most pleasant stretches of public ground in Britain—Jesus Green. Neither an enamelled display case for a cocktail-bibbing undergraduate élite nor an exclusive arbour for port-sodden dons, it is a genuine gathering-place for the whole community. It is also a parade ground for the kind of strutting clown who wants to let his Dobermann Pinscher out to play, while strenuously assuring you that there is no need for your child to be scared to death: Helmut would never dream of biting anyone. (Helmut never does, up until the moment when he inexplicably decides to chew a baby's face off.) But wait! Suddenly the giant hound pauses in its headlong flight, spreads its back legs and voids a rancid coil! Another pint of worms for the communal sewer. How much more shit can Britain take before it buckles under the strain and goes down like Atlantis?

6 July, 1975

The hard taskmasters

APPORTIONED between two successive Tuesday evenings, *The Final Solution: Auschwitz* (Thames) had more time than its parent episode in *The World at War* to make sense of its material. Within certain limits the programme did a good job. It looked inadequate only when attempting the impossible.

Further efforts were made towards presenting some of the mountain of original footage which research had gathered in for *The World at War*. A black-and-white phantasmagoria, the stuff made hideous viewing, even though it had been edited for contemplation rather than for shock. The programme wound its chronological way through the Thousand Year Reich from the first SS torch-light rallies to the ultimate paroxysms of the Nazis' self-imposed 'task'. There were clips or stills from most of the staging posts along their demented path. Where visual documentation ended – within the camps – there were interviews with participants.

Spokesmen for those who had suffered were well chosen. As the Eichmann trial demonstrated, witnesses who, usually for good reason, can't achieve some kind of emotional distance, however small, from an extreme experience can in the end do little to revivify it. The few interviewed by the programme were mainly either dispassionate or epigrammatic. One of them was outright funny. There was a solitary woman, out of the thousands still alive, who showed how she felt when her child was taken away. That was enough, or rather all that was useful, since if we couldn't draw the proper conclusions from her grief then multiplying it by any number – even by the number of similar mothers dead – would not help us.

Irony was kept well at bay. There is so much irony lying around this particular stretch of history that it would take a fool not to detect it, and a bigger fool to think it needed bringing out. Considering that the victims, when they arrived at the extermination camps, were ordered into showers which turned out to be gas-chambers, it was a cosmic irony to discover that a propaganda film of 1944, snappily entitled *Hitler Has Given the Jews a City* and aimed at tempting the helpless unprotestingly to their doom, featured a sequence in which happy people took showers. This was literally beyond a joke – a point which the commentary mercifully saw no necessity for making.

There was more of Himmler's boy assistant Hans Wolff, the unintentional comic turn of the *World at War* episode. Perhaps it isn't enough to thank our lucky stars that we weren't victims. We ought to thank them that we weren't Wolff, who is the walking embodiment of Hannah Arendt's much-misunderstood thesis that evil is banal – by which she meant that we ought to ask ourselves about the ordinary people who get mixed up in perpetrating it, rather than about the obvious monsters. Wolff is so ordinary he's phenomenal, still full of the 'difficulties' of the 'task'.

In Part Two Wolff told the story of Himmler's famous trip to Minsk. Himmler made Wolff watch a mass execution by shooting. Himmler got a spurt of blood on his uniform, turned green and waxed eloquent about the 'hard task'. It is difficult to know what to make of Himmler and the programme sensibly didn't preoccupy itself with sorting him out. He was terrifically mad, but then so are a lot of the people in mad-houses. Madness is quite ordinary, so the banality-of-evil theory remains unshaken. What was slightly unusual was to find an utter maniac running the police apparatus of a modern State.

Such questions were the responsibility of the commentary. *The World at War* was generally greeted by the critics as a distinguished series. Despite the sheer brilliance of its research I thought it rather less than that, principally because the commentary fudged points. There is a way of being simple while keeping faith with the complexity of events. Terse writing can do it. But *The World at War* commentary usually achieved only elision when it strove for compression, was too often simplistic rather than simple, and paradoxically sounded long-winded even at its most taciturn. The thing just wasn't written very well.

The commentary of *The Final Solution* was much nearer the mark. The necessary minimum of information was readily forthcoming. There is an inherent distortion in reducing twelve years of grief to a couple of hours of television, but granted that it's worth trying, this was the way to do it, although certain consequences followed inexorably. Chief among these was that the word 'Auschwitz' was further reinforced as a Duckspeak tag for the whole multiform experience.

Only once did a map appear showing the full extent of what has usefully been called the Concentrated Universe.

Auschwitz was a big piece of it but not by any means all, and to encourage the use of that one name as an emblem is to engage in the mental equivalent of haplography. Since a poet as serious as Robert Lowell has done the same thing in his poetry, I suppose the process is inevitable, but there's no reason to be happy about it.

Still, with all that said, the commentary did well, even with the awkward question of why the Jewish councils co-operated. When the voice-over started talking about 'too little concerted opposition' I thought for a giddy moment that the day was lost, but the point was soon amplified into 'people either didn't care enough, or were intimidated', and after that the crucial datum was made more and more clear —i.e., that the intimidation was unanswerable. The place to resist was in the ghetto, before the journey to oblivion began: but the S.S. had a way with ghettos that resisted.

The central moment of the programme came after an interview with an S.S. man called Richard Böck. A caption stating that he had refused to engage in the killing despite all threats of punishment was screened in silence long enough for us to make of the information what we could. My own conclusion was that Böck was a hero and that it is useless to expect the mass of men to behave like heroes. We should do our best to guard free institutions and not expect people to improve.

Regarded in this light, the commentary's more sententious statements were pious rhetoric. 'Auschwitz is history. Racial intolerance still persists.' Of course it does, and always will. 'We all have a responsibility to see that no one builds another Auschwitz.' On the contrary, we should devote ourselves to preserving more immediate freedoms, resisting in the ghetto. Responsibility begins and ends with what one can hope to achieve. But on the whole the programme was a lot less self-confidently minatory than that. It was written and directed by Michael Darlow.

24 August, 1975

Language games

'I DID NOT succeed to watch the television,' explained the French student in the first episode of Michael Frayn's *Making Faces* (BBC2). 'The last weekend I did not succeed to do nothing.'

'Anything,' said his English language teacher, Eleanor Bron. 'No,' he insisted. 'Anything is *not* what I did not. *Nothing* is what I did not.' Such elementary confusion at the language barrier amounts to a holiday for Frayn's characters, whose most anxiety-ridden dealings with English grammar and syntax take place within their own consciousness: it is in talking to themselves that they teeter at the cliff of unmeaning.

'It's not the effect that you have on me that worries me,' Bron explains to her boyfriend, who might as well not be there, 'it's the effect that I have on you. Or rather, it's the effect that the effect I have on you has on me.' (I think I noted that down correctly.) Frayn is deeply and continuously concerned with Wittgenstein's philosophy, especially in its later phases, when the subject became language games, leading to brain-boggling speculations about the prospect of a game without rules.

No great joker himself, Wittgenstein had an unfortunate effect on his sober-sided epigoni, whose commentaries on his work tended to sound as if Eleanor Bron dictated them under the hair-dryer. One recalls that G. E. M. Anscombe, in her introduction to one of the master's posthumous volumes, asks why, if it is informative to point out that the morning star is the same as the evening star, is it uninformative to point out that the evening star is the same as the evening star. Just such questions preoccupy the Frayn/Bron characters as their super-civilised minds slither over the brink of tears into the abyss.

Frayn's ideal aim in the drama has always been to load its rifts with the same ore that jammed every cranny of the novel *Towards the End of the Morning* and the columns collected in *The Book of Fub*, *At Bay in Gear Street* and *The Day of the Dog*. In his latest play for the theatre, *Alphabetical Order*, he took a large step towards attaining this end, but at the last I thought he had not quite done his faculty of invention justice – from Frayn one wants *wild* subtlety. After two episodes, *Making Faces* shows abundant signs of that, without endangering Frayn's determined repudiation of any atavistic retreat to the status of what he once called Jokey Man. (Jokey Man could have little to say about F. R. Leavis, the subject of the second episode, and one which it needs a sense of seriousness to take humorously.) Frayn has the mature humorist's horror of gags to no purpose. It is not a case of the clown wanting to play Hamlet, since Frayn was never a clown. The desire is to carry the comic vision through to its consequences, following E. M. Forster's dictum that art must be pursued to extremes.

John Cleese, who was and is a clown, might seem an unlikely figure to be afflicted with the same wish, but he is. He also shares Frayn's obsession with semantic fatigue, a fact lavishly attested to by his new series *Fawlty Towers* (BBC2), whose second episode – I did not succeed to watch the first – several times had me retching with laughter. There is a Spanish waiter perpetually on hand for the specific purpose of failing to understand what Cleese is talking about. '*Cuando nosotros somos* away ... away. What's "away" in Spanish?' Cleese asks the Spaniard, on that fierce note of hatred which in his case invariably precedes a paroxysm of violence – a fugue of aggro that devastates his immediate environment simply by the intensity with which it turns in upon itself, like an atomic pile in the throes of a melt-down. In this condition he sinks floorwards, knees together, feet a fathom apart, screaming through his ears while his clenched teeth spit chips of enamel, one fist smashing remorselessly into his own ribs while bloody fingernails appear through the knuckles of the other.

The common reader would be justified in finding the *Radio Times* article on the Cambridge of Frayn and Bron (written by Claire Tomalin, herself a famous alumna) kind of cosy. When you consider that Cleese went to the same place, I might be appearing to thicken the miasma of mutual admiration by suggesting that these enterprising talents are linked by the influence of the dear Varsity's salient modern thinker. No such intention: the truth is more mundane. The thing that joined them all up was the Footlights Dramatic Society — an institution which needs demystifying, since even in its various heydays it was never more than a place for histrionic neurotics to seek one another out. But since a certain percentage of them were intelligent histrionic neurotics, and since a certain percentage of those were talented intelligent histrionic neurotics, the effects have sometimes been far-reaching, especially when initial success in revue has faced the multi-qualified graduate with the problems of choosing what to do next.

Jonathan Miller, as seen on an unusually interesting *Parkinson* (BBC1), was the ex-Cambridge revue-star to the life and *in excelsis*. Telling the story of how his stutter made introducing *Monitor* an assault-course over nets and ponds of consonants, Miller couldn't help being wonderfully funny. Parky was perfectly right to ask him why he had given up making people laugh. And Miller was no doubt right in his turn to reply that the rigmarole of *preparing* to make people laugh ended by boring him.

Miller's co-interviewee was the admirable Lee Remick, who spoke concisely about the importance of the word 'No' in a performer's career. She is an instructive example of how intelligence in an actress can be penalised and yet survive, as opposed to the more numerous examples of the lack of it being rewarded and yet destroyed.

BBC2's new arts-fest *Arena* began absorbingly with

Kenneth Tynan asking Lord Olivier about Lilian Baylis. 'She is sometimes accused of being rude, mean, conceited. Did you find that?' 'Well ... yes.' On the *Book Programme* (BBC2) friends of Evelyn Waugh gathered at the Ritz to tell tales reinforcing his super-shit image. 'If he wanted to bully a few people it didn't bother *me*', said Ian Fleming's widow, setting us straight.

5 October, 1975

Very Peter Hall

THE new *Aquarius* (LWT) is very Peter Hall, very Sanderson.

With a distinctly royal air (very Peter Hall, very Sandringham) the show's new moderator hands down instruction to the natives (very Peter Hall, very Sanders of the River) concerning the contents of his sack of cultural goodies (very Peter Hall, very Santa Claus), revealing himself the while as perhaps deficient in humour (very Peter Hall, very sanctimonius) yet tireless in plugging the National Theatre (very Peter Hall, very sandwich-man). In short, the Peter Hall Glorification Virus is once again raging unchecked: vowing not to abet its activities even inadvertently, I have already mentioned his name seven times in two paragraphs, so insidious is the disease.

Hall is a man of great abilities, but needs more often to be told that he is mortal. At the Pope's coronation a man walks in front scattering dust, reminding the new prince that the glories of this world will come to nothing. It was a bit *ex cathedra* for Hall to disown the rather funny tour of Rome contributed by Russell Harty and Gore Vidal: the programme is *supposed* to feature items that don't reflect his views — it isn't necessarily a matter for universal alarm when somebody says something in his presence that he doesn't agree with. On the other hand, there was an impressive reading by Seamus Heaney: the show promises to retain all its familiar mixed blessings.

Meanwhile the Old Aquarian Humphrey Burton is managing Arts at the BBC, where his new policies are by now showing effect. He fronts *Omnibus* (BBC1) in person. Since the first episode of *Aquarius*, which he linked from a script falling apart in his trembling hands, Humph has come all the way across the galaxy, until he is now a consummate talking head. Chin in chest and peeking winningly upward through the top rung of his horn-rims, he is both boyishly tentative and internationally clued-up. The new presenters on *Film Night* (BBC2) should watch him in action and learn how to relax on television: two guys and a gal, they look (especially the guys) as if they are facing a firing squad.

Not that the old hands on *Arena* (BBC2) are doing much better. In the first instalment Kenneth Tynan read the autocue as if it contained a threatening letter from somebody else instead of a script written by himself, and in the second instalment—devoted to the visual arts—George Melly was stuck square in a tight head-shot and gave his usual impersonation of a man whose body, while he talks, is being slowly devoured by tiny fish. Melly needs to be stretched on a divan with a bunch of grapes in his hand before he gives full value on the box: he must have room to rave, and be encouraged to speak the unspeakable.

The new *Tonight* (BBC1) is not really that much more trivial than the old one. Programmes get idealised in retrospect, but even the dewiest-eyed would probably admit that the lovely Sue Lawley and her team, though barely adding up to a single authoritative personality, are nevertheless models of *gravitas* compared to Cliff Michelmore. What rankles is the extent to which all concerned with the new programme lack the *talent* for trivia. The secret of treating the kind of story which Murray Sayle immortalised

under the headline HEN LAYS 4″ EGG is to draw out its impli-
cations, connect it to the world.

But to want all that is to want the moon. What we
mostly get is the opposite capacity: instead of minor items
becoming stories, major stories become items. Still, there is
the odd bon-bon. The show got lucky last Monday night
when it happened to have a long compilation on the Cater-
ham bombing all set for the screen on the very day when
two men were picked up in Northern Ireland to be ques-
tioned on that very topic. Methods of detection were gone
into in some, although not exhaustive, detail: we never did
learn the exact characteristics proving that various bombs
were built by the same dab hand. But it was interesting to
see how the miniature reconstruction of the pub (Action-
Man and Barbie-Doll puppets placed according to scores
of patiently elicited memories from the survivors) revealed
the presence of two strangers.

Everybody seems to be pro-police again now that the
Evil One is so patently on the loose. The *Philpott File* (BBC2)
has devoted several highly watchable programmes to the
fuzz, who emerged as a body of men so reassuringly staunch
that it was hard not to burst into tears of gratitude. Aspirants
to the rank of Inspector had their minds broadened by being
told that although 'public order problems are going to get
bigger', things like soccer hooliganism and 'the flying picket
situation' had a social basis. Whether telling or being told,
all concerned looked a lot smarter than Harry the Hawk. In
the latest episode we saw the top men. The Chief Constable
of Surrey came across as a superbly groomed, inspiringly
capable father-figure—a combination of Peter Hall and
God, without the latter's limitations.

Celebrating Kenneth More's forty years in show-biz, *A
Little More, Please* (Thames) was a classic. The luckless
guest of honour at the adulatory feast was first of all shown
journeying nervously towards the venue in the back of a
large car, while his own voice-over gave us his thoughts in a

stream of semi-consciousness. 'Forty years in show business. And I have to face them all today. An ego-trip, I suppose ... What have I *done* with my forty years? I've made some mistakes. Six months in India with David Lean, the greatest director in the world ... '

In position at the site, luminaries queued to endorse Pete Murray's paean for 'Kenny's happy-go-lucky personality.' Dilys Powell was intent on conveying that Kenny was 'very English. He's always been a very *English* actor.' This dispelled any lingering doubts that he might have been a very Chinese actor, but aroused the suspicion that he might not be remarkable for range. 'He's always been the same,' said Geoffrey Keen, meaning it as praise.

Pete asked Douglas Bader how it had felt to see Kenny impersonating him in *Reach for the Sky*. 'Totally unreal,' Bader replied, and this also was meant as praise. A speech from Harry Secombe, however, managed to inject a note of intentional humour. And since Secombe is a man incapable of dissimulation, it followed that More must really be as nice and kind as everybody said, despite the way they chose to say it.

A wall of corn from Cornwall, BBC1's new thriller serial *Poldark* is aptly branded with a title which turns out to be an anagram for Old Krap. I rest my case.

12 October, 1975

Schmlittering prizes

THE first in a series of six plays about 'fifties Cambridge written by Frederic Raphael under the collective title of *The Glittering Prizes* (BBC2), 'An Early Life' starred Tom Conti as an energetic, sensitive, witty and passionate student, singled out by his Jewishness and alacrity of mind.

From the ample pre-publicity there were good reasons to think that Frederic Raphael had based this central character on himself. Whatever the truth of that, Adam Morris (for so the pivotal figure in the play was named, 'Frederic Raphael' having presumably been judged too direct) was certainly a good subject for a *Bildungsroman* – or would have been, had he not arrived in Cambridge with his *Bildung* already completed.

Normally there is no juicier topic than a bright young man coming up to university and getting his education. But Adam Morris seemed to have got his in the sixth form, leaving him nothing to do with his Cambridge days except (a) make the odd pardonable mistake, and (b) lose his virginity. The odd pardonable mistake lay in underestimating the nasty-looking aristocratic mother of his dying room-mate; from her he learned a lesson in self-denial. He lost his virginity, with enviable lack of fuss, to a beautiful student teacher.

Apart from these events, which were doubtless formative in their different ways, Adam was already uncannily intact – sardonic, wise, mature. He was crass about attacking people's religious faith, but you could see his reasons. Otherwise he had the aphoristic subtlety of Montaigne. There seemed small reason for his being a student at all. He should have been doing the teaching. Cambridge, for better or for worse, is a place where young people grow and change. Adam was above that. Tom Conti played Adam in a style reminiscent of Peter Sellers pretending to be a lounge-lizard. So tentative and inwardly giggling a manner half-worked when Conti was being Madame Bovary's husband last year, but didn't work at all when he was being energetic, sensitive, witty and passionate, singled out by his Jewishness and alacrity of mind. When not emitting one of the clever things Frederic Raphael once said (or else *would* have said, but thought of too late, and so is saying now), Conti conveyed introspection by encouraging his eyes to glisten wetly, while smiling with secret knowledge.

147

The hard-to-take hero would have mattered less if the play built around him had given you more idea of what Cambridge in that period was actually like. Doubtless future episodes will. But here, in the instalment that was meant to set the tone, there was precious little sense of anything special going on – and 'fifties Cambridge, after all, was the time and place when all the hot-shots who have since dominated the media were getting to know one another. They were, or if they weren't they are, self-consciously a Generation.

Only the contemporary habit of imitating Bluebottle's voice gave us a sense of time, which was promptly undone by showing us a list of names on a St John's College staircase done in Letraset instead of hand-painted. The sense of place was most conspicuously given by inviting the mastaba of the University library, the most hideous building in Cambridge, to loom in the background. (E. M. Forster has an excellent essay listing all the vantage points from which it can't be seen.)

Nor were the epigrams any great shakes. Reviewing a book by Michael Frayn, Mr Raphael once talked about the Cambridge trick of smiling to recruit someone's intellectual assent, and being intelligent to recruit his affection. This might have been a pseudo-observation (why isn't it an Oxford trick, or an Aberystwyth trick?), but I could have stood for a few like it in the script. And instead of conflating and disguising the real-life illuminati, it might have been more evocative simply to name them, or even give them identity tags. A dull start.

Clayhanger (ATV) is so-so: better than bad, but less than a knock-out. A lot of it takes place around the dinner table. People like to watch actors eat (Ferenc Molnar wrote a whole play based on this principle) but there are limits. When the action moves elsewhere, the series looks under-budgeted: the Five Towns are less grimy than tatty, with lanes and alleys laid suspiciously flat and walls that shake if you lean against them. Until Janet Suzman arrived in episode three, Harry Andrews as old Darius Clayhanger had to carry the burden, or can, of being the salient figure. A doddle for him, since all he had to do was rant, but tiresome for us. Young Edwin, even though by episode four he had grown up enough to be played by Peter McEnery, was never in the running as the centre of excitement. It was from Hilda Lessways that the boost had to come if the show was to achieve orbit.

It hasn't happened. Janet Suzman can work every miracle except looking callow. Trying to be that, she is arch. As the series progresses through time she will become more credible, but at the moment we have to watch the most womanly of women pretending to be girlish, which she does by crooking her elbows and talking with a coy trill. If she had less presence, she might get away with it.

On *Read All About It* (BBC1), A. J. Ayer indulged his bad habit of saying 'Mm, mm' impatiently while other people spoke, as if their points were too obvious to require putting. I found this wonderfully unendearing. Lord Chalfont, fronting *Who Says It Could Never Happen Here?* (Anglia) was also on characteristic form. Aided by Anthony Lejeune, Lord Shawcross and similar deep thinkers, he warned of the Communist threat to democracy. The warnings sounded like a threat to democracy in themselves. Lord Shawcross said that the next 'five or fifteen years' would see a totalitarian Government installed in Britain – probably a Communist one. So in four or fourteen years it'll be time to get your skates on.

25 January, 1976

A Muggeridge fragment

IN *A Third Testament* (BBC2), Malcolm Muggeridge was on about Kierkegaard, whose opinions he found much to his taste, especially the one about the masses being wrong, even when what they say is right. Kierkegaard was used as a stick with which to beat Marx, who was supposed to have initiated the folly of thinking numerically. A dispassionate observer might have pointed out that one of Marx's reasons for writing as he did was out of revulsion at the inhumanity of industrialists who were already thinking numerically on their own account. But Muggeridge's late-flowering spirituality is beyond such considerations. He even managed to convince himself that Kierkegaard shared his contempt for television, presumably by clairvoyance. To appear on television and explain the futility of television to the masses whose opinion is not worth having – truly this is the work of a saint.

1 February, 1976

Unintelligibühl

'IF WE ate what we listened to,' said the pianist *Earl Wild* (BBC2), 'we'd all be dead.' He meant Muzak, but his observation applied equally well to the English language, which in this week's television received a fearful bashing from more than one direction.

For example, there was NATO Supreme Commander General Alexander Haig, talking to Robin Day on *Newsday* (BBC2). General Haig looks the way a general ought to look, with a Steve Canyon countenance, shoulders like an armoured personnel carrier, and rows of medal ribbons running down one side of his chest and out of the picture. Unfortunately he sounds like nothing on earth. It is almost impossible to understand him, since he crams so many polysyllabic abstractions into a sentence that he forgets the beginning before he reaches the end.

Quizzed by Robin on the Soviet military build-up, General Haig squared his jaw and talked of the restructured multi-capable inter-parity situation of the SALT ceiling. Robin adjusted his glasses and rephrased his question. General Haig squared his jaw even further and rephrased his answer, talking of how the shortfall in assessment of the balanced triad necessitated that he participate in the evolution of viable agreement postures.

Apart from hitting General Haig in the face with a custard-pie, there wasn't a lot Robin could do except plough on. If the West was going broke, how could it meet the Russian threat? General Haig squared his jaw to the point of crystalline fatigue failure and gave answer. The United States no longer wielding hegemonial power in the tightly interdependent global strategic environment, the NATO allies in the present socio-economic crisis situation would require to keep their perspectives clear. Robin, looking as if he had been wrestling a mattress full of treacle, retired defeated. General Haig looked triumphant. Now for the Russians.

'John Curry pulled out *everything!*' screamed Alan Weeks in *Olympic Grandstand* (BBC1). So did the BBC commentators. For them, Innsbruck was a kind of apotheosis. What would the Winter Olympics be without them?

To start with, it would be literate — but let's not carp. We've done that before. In the sweet instant of an unarguable British victory, it behoves us to be proud, and that includes being proud of Alan Weeks, Ron Pickering, David Vine and David Coleman. Vine, especially, is a changed man. Not once did he lapse into a repetition of the unforgettable moment when he predicted that an athlete would shortly pull out the big one. He left that to Alan Weeks, who on the evening of the pairs figure-skating final duly delivered himself of a classic. 'This might well be the night', mused Alan, 'when Rodnina pulls everything out.' Thereby confirming our suspicions about Russian female athletes.

Coleman, Weeks, Pickering and Vine all made copious use of this year's official BBC demonstrative adjective, this. This man, this is the man, this girl, this is the girl. The ski-ing ability of Klammer was referred to as 'the brilliance of this man'. There were several instances of last year's the man who, as in 'The man who was injured last year', but they were overwhelmed by the popularity of this is the man who, as in 'This is the man who challenged Thoeni at Burble Valley.'

This is the man who was sometimes shortened to this the man who, as in 'This the man who leads the commatition.' For some reason, this advanced form was never used when referring to women, who were still sometimes the girl who (as in 'The girl who lives in the tiny village of Unintelligi-bühl'), were very often this is the girl who (as in 'This is the girl from Gruntstadt in Mumblestein who fractured an ovary at Grenoble'), but were never this the girl who.

Why this should be was a difficult question. This the question that was difficult to answer. While you were working on it, there were some nice things to watch. I liked the American pairs skaters, anglo Randy Gardner and ethnic Tai Babilonia. Super-Wasp and the Half-Breed! As usual, Irena Rodnina carried on like a ballbreaker, in-cinerating Zaitsev with her beetle-browed hate-stare when he got his blades tangled. It will be a relief when those two retire from commatition, since for all their technical razzle-dazzle they are unpoetic to the last degree. Not that Rodnina lacks femininity compared to some other members of the Russian team. One of their speed-skating persons bore a startling resemblance to Johnny Weissmuller. Perhaps it was thinking about her which led Reginald Bosanquet on *News at Ten* (ITN) to mention an event called the 500 kilometres women's speed-skating.

If you can accept the fact that *Bouquet of Barbed Wire* (LWT) is the house of Atreus transferred to Peyton Place on a long low loader, there are worse serials to get hooked on. It won't rot your brains like *The Brothers*. Nor will you see – as in so many other series currently on the screen – the roof of a coal-mine fall on the hero's father. Instead there is plenty of solid middle-class adultery and incest. Sheila Allen is having a whale of a time as the Older Woman who has welcomed her daughter's husband into her bed, which is roughly what her husband (Frank Finlay) would like to do with the daughter, and perhaps will, or even perhaps once did, or perhaps both.

I have been unfair to *When the Boat Comes In* (BBC1), which has really been far too good to ignore. James Bolam is quite superb in the leading role. But I was sad to see, in the latest episode, the roof of a coal-mine fall on the hero's father. It is one of the few blessings of *Clayhanger* (ATV) that the series is set in the Potteries, thus ruling out the possibility that the roof of a coal-mine will fall on the hero's father. There is always the chance, I suppose, that a kiln will instead.

I hate to go on and on about *The Brothers* (BBC1), but it's turning into a very freaky scene. It looks as if Jenny is scheduled for the funny farm. That's where Brian went when they wrote him out for a whole series. When he came back, he had a moustache. When Jenny comes back, will she have one too? If there is no room at the asylum, she could always become one of the presenters of *Terra Firma* (BBC2): there are three already, and might as well be four, since the main interest of this new magazine programme's first instalment lay in watching the cooks crowd round the broth.

Ned Sherrin, a genuinely sharp character, could easily have run the whole show on his own, but had been burdened with help. Alasdair Clayre, fronting a thrill-a-minute story about canals, spoke in the tones of someone contemplating taking holy orders. Nemone Lethbridge was in charge of the standard item about stud bulls. There was a certain *frisson* in listening to her ritzy accent while her elegant hand patted a bull's bum, but the news was stale – which didn't, of course, stop *Nationwide* (BBC1) covering the same topic all over again a few nights later.

15 February, 1976

Standing at the window

'I N an hour's time,' said the ITV link-man, 'we've got some professional wrestling. But let's meet some people now who are wrestling ... with life.' *Breakdown* (Granada), an interesting play by Julian Bond, went out in the 'Wednesday Special' slot, which is hardly peak time, but could have meant that a good proportion of the *News at Ten* audience who had been slow to go to bed during the subsequent commercials might have stuck around to watch the start of it. Watching the start was practically a guarantee of staying hooked till the end, since the course of the action was inexorable.

Jack Hedley played Ralph, an insurance broker forced to the edge of breakdown by the pressures of second mortgage, second woman, second mess. Sylvia (the second woman, ably played by Wanda Ventham) woke up in the middle of the night to discover Ralph standing at the window of their high-rise flat, talking of suicide. The following scene was mainly an extraordinarily well-sustained speech delivered by Hedley with the skill the writing deserved. You needn't have gone all the way to the brink yourself to see that this was just the way someone on the point of a crack-up would talk, if he could talk at all.

Needless to say, Sylvia didn't quite realise the magnitude of the problem. Nobody ever does, which is why you have to have the breakdown, to tell everyone that it's not a matter of being reasonable or seeing things in proportion – it's a matter of getting *all* the pressures off, *now*. 'My poor, poor love. Come to bed,' cooed Sylvia, but it wasn't enough. A pair of friends were called in to offer reasonable advice, but that wasn't enough either. In fact it was while the friends were talking that Ralph flipped his wig. For Hedley this was the last big scene, since later on he was required to do no more than look dazed. He went spare wonderfully, his mouth going all rectangular like a crying baby's. Watching him was a rough ride.

Sylvia reluctantly committed Ralph into the care of a blunt but *simpatico* medico who didn't talk down either to her or to us, which made him almost unique in screen history. But the pressure of seeing Ralph make no apparent progress soon started telling on Sylvia in her turn, so that she was in a bad way herself by the time he was finally allowed out, with her job in jeopardy and no assurance that the same thing wouldn't happen all over again. In the last scene *she* was standing at the window – thus completing a neatly circular construction, without allowing us to think that anything had been resolved.

Bond captured with praiseworthy accuracy the way someone who abruptly finds everything too much retreats to simple decisions and then can't even manage those. It's the near-vertical steepness of the gradient that makes the decline so memorable. Unfortunately (and this the play didn't touch on) letting go is also kind of fun, which is why some unscrupulous people fake it, spoiling the market for the rest of us.

22 February, 1976

Solzhenitsyn warns the West

IN a week's television not otherwise notable for moral content, Alexander Solzhenitsyn (*Panorama*, BBC1) bulked large. He was interviewed by Michael Charlton, who probably did as good a job as was possible, considering that there is no way of extracting Solzhenitsyn's message in condensed form.

The interview was preceded by a lightning tour of Solzhenitsyn's career. A measure of his success in writing books which evoke recent Russian history in its full horrific force is that such summaries now seem hopelessly inadequate. In the interview proper Solzhenitsyn spoke Russian, with a translation dubbed over. This intensified, I found, the already slightly other-worldly feeling induced by his appearance, so evocative of both Lincoln and Dickens — men who spoke roundly on ethical issues, a largely vanished practice. That Solzhenitsyn should engage in such an old-fashioned activity is a reminder, difficult to assimilate, that the Soviet present branches off from somewhere in our past — it is a parallel universe, different and inimical. Talking to us about moral regeneration, he sounds like Dr Arnold of Rugby. A bit dated. After all, we've got beyond all that. We're all the way up to Hugh Hefner.

The question of Solzhenitsyn's pride in his mission was raised when he told Charlton that his personal experience was vital to the West but won't be understood by it. Knowing Solzhenitsyn's books reasonably well, I believe that he is being humble when he speaks like this, but I can easily see how he might appear the opposite, especially to those who will be basing their opinions of him on watching *Panorama* rather than knuckling down to the admittedly formidable task of reading his collected works.

What Solzhenitsyn means here, I think, is not that he is

some lofty exemplar of a difficult principle (later in the interview he repeatedly rejected Charlton's suggestion that he might see himself as a redeemer, an anti-Lenin) but that historical lessons can't be transmitted intact. He makes it clear in *Gulag Archipelago* Volume 1 that he has no faith in the ability of the truth to propagate itself automatically, even under ideal conditions of freedom. His remarkable humility consists in addressing himself with such heroic resolve to a task of which he has no false expectations.

Solzenhitsyn declared himself unable to comprehend how the West can possess freedom and not value it. This was a telling rhetorical point but as a tenet in his position — which it is, recurring throughout his work — it has some awkward logical consequences. For example, if freedom is valued most when it is nearest to being extirpated, and least when it is most prevalent, then perhaps freedom needs to be threatened in order to be conscious of itself. It's a high price to pay for consciousness.

There is no possibility of over-valuing freedom, but there is the possibility of valuing it wrongly, and I think that to a certain extent Solzhenitsyn does so. He is on sure ground when he warns against tyranny but weak ground when he laments that liberty has not made us morally aware. Liberty can't do that: political freedom means nothing unless it is extended to those who are incapable of valuing it. Warning the West against the East, Solzhenitsyn can hope to be of some effect. Warning the West against itself, he is surely addressing himself to the wrong object. The West lacks a common moral purpose *because* it is free, so there is no point in his attacking our lack of moral purpose unless he attacks freedom too.

Similarly, his doctrine concerning the undividable nature of freedom has awkward consequences for his line of argument about what the West should do. It might well be that the Soviet Union will attempt to dominate the world. But that doesn't mean we should allow ourselves to be repressed

by our own leaders in order that the threat might be coun-
tered – not if we believe that freedom is undividable. For
the West, the political meaning of the Vietnam war lay
in the refusal of an American generation to let its Govern-
ment subvert the Constitution by suppressing specific
freedoms in the name of an allegedly greater good. In the
eye of history, which does not take sides, this might well
prove to have been part of a disastrous chain of events in
which the West destroyed itself by trying to preserve its free
institutions.

But my point is that Solzhenitsyn can't have it both ways.
One of the great lessons of his life and work is that the only
thing ensured by giving up freedoms for a greater good is
that the greater good will be evil when it arrives and the
freedoms will be impossible to retrieve. To be worried about
the K.G.B. doesn't mean that we should stop being worried
about the C.I.A. In fact being worried about the C.I.A. is
probably the most effective way of being worried about the
K.G.B., since the West will never be able to defeat totali-
tarianism by going totalitarian – it will always arrive second
– but might possibly stand a chance by remaining liberal.

Talking of the West's imminent collapse, Solzhenitsyn is
paradoxically enrolling himself in a millenarian tradition
which includes Marx. He is likely to be no better than his
forerunners at predicting history. Solzhenitsyn's strength –
his majestic strength – lies in his capacity to recover the past.
He is the survivor of an historical catastrophe so violent that
it would be understandable if he were no longer sane. And
yet when you look at what he has achieved, the first thing
that strikes you is the human tone, the lack of messianic rant.

Primus inter pares in what he called on *Panorama* the 'fight
for our memory', he is at one with comparably brave
writers like Evgenia Ginzburg and Nadezhda Mandelstam
in being true to what he knows, and beyond them in being
able to extend that personal awareness to what he did not
himself experience. He has given facts the force of imagina-

tion and made history a work of art, while being aware that a work of art is the most intense possible revelation of the assumptions which inform it. As he said in his Nobel Lecture, 'conceptions which are devised or stretched do not stand being portrayed in images, they all come crashing down, appear sickly and pale, convince no one. But those works of art which have scooped up the truth and presented it to us as a living force – they take hold of us, compel us, and nobody ever, not even in ages to come, will appear to refute them.'

7 March, 1976

The QB VII *travesty*

SPREADING over two evenings, *QB VII* (BBC1) was a mammoth American opus about Hitler's destruction of the European Jews. Done from the heart, with no expense spared – everybody from Lee Remick to Sir John Gielgud walked through – this was a television programme which was not afraid to plumb the depths of the human spirit. Not afraid, and not qualified.

The title was a tip-off. Big bad novels often have numbers for titles, market research having revealed that browsing yokels respond to figures rather than to letters when seeking out an easy read. Hence *Butterfield 8, Catch–22, Slaughterhouse 5, Mila 18* – the last being the work of Leon Uris, who indeed also wrote the novel *QB VII*, from which one Edward Anhalt drew the tele-play for the programme under discussion. QB VII is apparently the standard abbreviation for Queen's Bench No. 7 of the Law Courts, London, where Uris and Anhalt pretended that a Dr Sir Adam Kelno sued a Jewish novelist called Abraham Cady for libel after Cady had imputed that Kelno performed hideous operations on

Jews in concentration camps. With many excursions through time to explore the personalities of Kelno and Cady, the story-line unfolded in the courtroom.

Shorn of the flashbacks, the trial scenes would have worked well enough. In fact they had done so once before, when a much smaller programme on the same subject was made in England, its script based closely on a trial which actually took place, with Uris involved. Uris and Anhalt took the same real-life event as their departure point, but in adding their own explanations did a far more effective job than their less ambitious predecessor of leaving the matter in the dark.

The script throughout was worthy and giftless, like the dialogue put into the actors' mouths in the star-strewn film *Judgment at Nuremberg*, another big bad production on the same theme, with an equally strident sense of mission. And just as, at the time, it was inadvisable to point out that *Judgment at Nuremberg* was a big bad movie without first laboriously establishing that you were not necessarily pro-Nazi, so now it is perhaps not wise to argue that *QB VII* was a big bad programme without also insisting that one is far from indifferent to the subject of the Holocaust. In fact one would like to believe oneself even more passionate on the topic than *QB VII*'s authors who, if they really understood its importance, would have had the grace to leave it alone, since their talents were patently not up to treating it.

From the first few minutes of the show, when the inmates of the concentration camps liberated in 1945 were described as 'pathetic scarecrows of human beings' you knew that nobody concerned with the production could write for nuts. However exalted in its aims, this was going to be hack-work. The casting was adequate in the leading roles – Ben Gazzara, who played Cady, and Anthony Hopkins, who played Kelno, are both good actors, although Hopkins increasingly took refuge in mannerism as the script left him high and dry – but the conceptions of character which the players

were asked to embody were hopelessly cliché-ridden, despite
everything the director, producer and writers could do to
make them profound. *Because* of everything they could do.

For the student of schlock (and schlock-merchants *always*
produce schlock, especially when they try to be sincere) the
role of Abraham Cady, successful Jewish novelist, was
especially revealing. Whether or not Mr Uris identified with
him, Cady was a classic example of the Hollywood writer's
fantasies about Integrity and Talent. For much of the first
part of the show he was to be seen barging about spilling
drinks, consumed with self-disgust at writing bad books.
It is *de rigueur* in this fantasy for the writer to suppose that he
writes bad books through choice, and that if he could only
reject the swimming-pool and recover his Integrity he
would be able to write good ones. It rarely occurs to him –
certainly it never seemed to occur to Cady – that he writes
bad books because he is a bad writer.

At the end of Part I, Cady, consumed by self-loathing and
shattered by the collapse of his marriage, went to Jerusalem,
where he visited the Yad Vashem Memorial, at last grasped
what the Nazis did to his people, and recovered his Integrity
along with his faith. 'I know what I have to write about
now,' he gritted, with the sub-*Exodus* soundtrack music
welling in the background. 'I want the reader to be there
when they haul up the Star of David over Jerusalem and
rekindle the Sacred Flame. I pray that God gives me the
Talent to do it.' In Part II, God came through with the
goods.

The problem was left in abeyance of how we could
possibly respect Cady as a writer, if he had to recover his
faith before he found out what Nazi Europe had been like.
What on earth had he thought before? The universal
catastrophe of ideological genocide was reduced to a
specious conflict in the mind of a Hollywood mediocrity.
The few powerful scenes could only emphasise this central
inadequacy, although they did lift the show a notch above

Judgment at Nuremberg, which left a generation of young cinema-goers with the impression that the Nazi regime did bad things to Judy Garland.

Chronicle (BBC2), hosted by Magnus Magnusson, featured a Danish family voluntarily returning to Iron Age conditions. 'A box of matches was the only concession to the twentieth century,' Magnus explained, as the Bjornholts squatted around the quern and ground the draves with a splon. The nubile Bjornholt daughters glumly bared their bosoms to the Iron Age breeze, thereby supplying the male viewer with an alternative centre of interest while their father chipped splinths. 'They settled into an Iron Age routine of making food and making fire,' said Magnus. The routine couldn't have been routiner. Killing a chicken counted as heavy action.

We were shown the uncannily well-preserved bodies of people who had supposedly been ritually slain and dumped in the bogs, although the possibility was hard to rule out that they had suicided to escape the Iron Age tedium. Then it was back again to Dad, striding purposefully around in hair pants on the trail of edible klud. It helped to fight off sleep if you counted how many other concessions there were to the twentieth century besides the matches, although perhaps Mum's dark glasses were authentic Iron Age artefacts, obtained from one of those caravans that blew in from Rome once every ten years with a cargo of beads.

2 May, 1976

Cant-struck

THE best documentary of the week was the second episode of *Spirit of '76* (BBC1), Julian Pettifer's trio of programmes about America. Concerned with marriage and divorce, this show was not quite as probing as the first, which had been about race – a less amorphous topic. Defeated in advance by the amount of solemn rhetoric the Americans attach to love, Pettifer unwisely sought assistance by filming a lengthy interview with one Dr Urie Bronfenbrenner, a super-bore billed as 'America's leading authority on the family'.

Dr Bronfenbrenner had a way of stating the obvious that glazed your eyeballs like crockery. Assembling tautologies at the rate of a small child getting dressed for school, he raised a wise finger to ram home phrases like 'ethic of confrontation'. His opening remarks were overwhelming evidence in support of the theory that the chief problem Americans face concerning sex lies in the language they use to talk about it.

A marriage-guidance radio programme hosted by 'Bill Balance and resident sexologist Dr Laura Schlesinger' at least had some speed. But as a rule glacial ponderosity prevailed. We saw a disintegrating couple in the hands of a counsellor. 'He looks at everything I do as naïve and stupid,' complained the wife, condemning herself out of her own mouth. 'I've changed my personality for you!' she moaned, piling Pelion on Ossa. Almost too bored to speak, the husband summoned the energy to observe: 'I might think you're dumber than I am in certain ways, but it's got nothing to do with how old you are.' At this point the counsellor intervened, speaking very clearly, so that both parties would be able to understand her. 'It seems clear to me', she enunciated, 'that the two of you aren't going to agree on this issue'.

This was where Pettifer should have thrust his head into shot and asked whether the concept of a private life can be said to exist at all, once married couples start inviting TV crews to a discussion of their personal griefs. But there was no time for contemplation: there was too much material. Onward to a group grope organised by Single Scene, a nationwide organisation for the lonely. People were shown feeling one another up. This was called a 'caring-type massage'. The various kinds of shack-up were grouped together under the heading of LTAs – 'living-together arrangements'.

In this miasma of sociological cant Pettifer had real trouble finding anyone intelligent enough to talk to: they were lobotomising themselves as fast as they spoke. A mother who had left her child at home so that she could come to a meeting about how to be a better mother worriedly announced that her child hadn't wanted her to come to the meeting. The constant assumption was that boredom and lack of love would turn into their opposites if you could find the right words.

23 May, 1976

Hoggart on class

A WEEK after the event at least one viewer is still chuckling at the sublime outrage with which Richard Hoggart, in an absorbing *Second House* on Class (BBC2), reacted to an old clip of John Betjeman (as he then was), Nevill Coghill, A. L. Rowse and Lord David Cecil sitting around in Oxford congratulating themselves on their own degree of civilisation.

In just such a fashion D. H. Lawrence had reacted to Bloomsbury, not so much because he was a Northern boy and the Bloomsberries were privileged, as because they weren't as clever as they thought they were but couldn't take the fact in when he pointed it out – they always thought he was moved by class animus. (Significantly it was Keynes who finally admitted that Lawrence had had a point. Keynes really *was* bright.) The Coghill *camarilla* airily discussing the basis of their own distinction – they were agreed that it was Oxford which gave them the opportunity to nurture their own excellence – were a diverting example of the same kind of complacency. Hoggart, another Northern boy, was simply echoing Lawrence's impatience with it.

Hoggart started to point out what was plainly a fact – that the claims these men were making for the intellectual productivity of Oxford were absurd – but there was no time to pursue the argument in the full richness of its potential. It really was marvellous to watch A. L. Rowse talking about the disinterested quest for Truth while his friends lolled about nodding wisely, forgetting to add or else never having noticed that for A. L. Rowse the Truth had usually been any foolish notion that happened to pop into his head.

You could say Betjeman had distinction, and all four men had undoubtedly seized the opportunities offered by Oxford to cultivate their eccentricities to the full, but that was about it. What we were looking at was not a concentration of mental power but a mutual admiration society – a club. And it was surely the knowledge that such clubs are still with us that led Hoggart ever so slightly to blow his cool.

For the rest of the programme he remained detached, but never less than interesting. The subject-matter consisted of excerpts from television programmes since the year dot. Melvyn Bragg, more abrasive lately, extracted Hoggart's opinions of the attitudes revealed by the murky old films and tapes as they spooled unsteadily past. Even where the attitudes were self-evident, the guest's opinions were still illuminating. In a 1956 *Panorama* Max Robertson interviewed two different lots of schoolboys about their future careers. One lot were from a secondary modern and the other from a grammar school.

There could be no doubt in the world about which group Robertson felt at home with. When one of the sec. mod. boys announced that he saw his future in 'tiling and slabbing' Robertson repeated the words as if, Hoggart observed, he were 'holding a dead fish out'.

An ancient programme called *Can You Tell Me?* featured a lady called Phyllis Digby Morton – who regrettably was before my time – handing out advice to the socially uneasy. Showing his rare gift for combining general argument with specific detail, Hoggart pinned down the show's genteel aspirations by identifying the lady's trick of saying 'deteriating' for 'deteriorating' as a mark of the upper classes. A 1957 extract from *The Grove Family* showed the Beeb still unable to reflect the class structure any way except unconsciously: the family had a caricature Northern grandma and a daughter from RADA.

Coronation Street was the big break-through, with observation helping to create believable types, if not individuals. Bragg and Hoggart were agreed that television nowadays did a much better job of showing what was actually going on in British society. A clip of Billy Connolly appearing on the *Parkinson* show vividly demonstrated the real life that was always waiting to be discovered once the fantasies had been cleared away. But, Hoggart warned, 'the reality of class has hardly changed.'

Perhaps he was right about the country at large, but in the land of the media – especially in television – class has altered radically. For example, here were Richard Hoggart and Melvyn Bragg up on the screen discussing the subject with each other, instead of having their opinions relayed to the audience through Max Robertson. Despite their lowly origins, they showed no sign of unease. If, as members of the communications élite, they could be said to belong to a new class, they certainly no longer belonged to any of the old ones. And if it was true that what was *on* television had changed, then things *in* television must have changed too, since it is axiomatic that there is never a significant alteration in what happens on screen without a proportionately large alteration of personnel behind it.

6 June, 1976

Larger than life

SELLING untold millions of pop records on the Continent and now starting to break big in this country also, Demis Roussos — fat, shaggy, rich, dynamic — is a Phenomenon. This was proved by the title of BBC2's show about him, *The Roussos Phenomenon.*

'What *is* the appeal of this larger than life-size entertainer?' the commentator asked himself worriedly. 'Does it lie in the man himself, or his music?' This was no easy question. Common sense dictated that the Phenomenon's appeal could not lie in his music, which is derivative to the point of putrefaction. But it seemed even less likely that the appeal could lie in the man himself, since the larger than life-size entertainer was quickly revealed as one of the least attractive showbiz Phenomena since Jimmy Boyd, the delinquent who saw Mommy kissing Santa Claus. His wealth, however, coupled with the hysterical devotion of his fans, argued that one must be wrong on both counts.

Described as 'an avid collector of precious metals' and as having 'a *pension* for furry robes,' the Phenomenon 'surrounds himself with the trappings of luxury' at his home in France. But really he is beyond materialism, enjoying things only for their spiritual essence. 'My bathroom can bring to you a certain atmosphere,' he explained, clomping around in silver platform boots behind a larger than life-size stomach.

His stage manner reflects the opulence of his domicile. There is an immense reserve of inner warmth, as in a compost heap. 'I would like to tell you a beautiful story now. A story about myself ... and a very beautiful friend of mine – the wind.' The band starts up, and while his guitarists are sorting out their chords the Phenomenon does a bit more talking. 'I meet my friend the wind, and he is telling me beautiful stories.' Then, when his musicians are finally all heading in more or less the same direction, the larger than life-size entertainer stops talking about his friend and starts to sing about him, or her.

The singing is done in an unrelenting yin-tong tremolo which would curdle your brains like paint-stripper if you gave it time. I did not, but switched off too late to avoid hearing the Phenomenon's valedictory sentiment: 'I think the most important thing in life is to be loved.' The people you most hate always do.

Bill Brand (Thames), a new series about a young Labour M.P. written by Trevor Griffiths and starring Jack Shepherd, will inevitably be compared with Arthur Hopcraft's *The Nearly Man*, but already looks like surviving the comparison well enough. Running out of things to say about a mature Labour M.P. with a debilitating *pension* for the high life, Hopcraft, to fill his scripts, was forced to rely on his friend the wind. (From this point I will eschew all further references to the Phenomenon, who got to me like hepatitis.) Griffiths is unlikely to run out of things to say about Brand, an immature Labour M.P., fresh from teaching liberal studies at the local tech, whose tastes run in the other direction, towards Clause 4 and the kind of principles which will undoubtedly bring him under heavy pressure from his own party whips. Disinclined to be mere lobby-fodder, Brand will attempt to turn a grim visage against compromise.

Jack Shepherd was ideal casting for the title role, since visages come no grimmer – possessing the only pair of sunken pop eyes in the business, he has always appeared to be just back from a long season in the Inferno. He is a very good naturalistic actor and Griffiths writes very good naturalistic dialogue, so the central performance is in the bag. Luckily, because on the evidence of the first episode, the drift of events could well be more than slightly towards the mono-chrome.

Like the Nearly Man, Brand is equipped with both wife and mistress, but since Brand's mistress is fully as dis-illusioned as the Nearly Man's wife, and since his wife is correspondingly twice as disillusioned as the mistress, it will be appreciated that Brand comes in for a lot of flak. 'You're an egotistical swine of a man,' Mrs Brand informs him helpfully on election night, 'you make me puke.' When Brand gets in with a reduced majority, the fact is registered in a reaction shot of the mistress watching television. She is underjoyed, presumably realising that she must now see even less of him. Thus it is that Brand makes the big stride from Manchester to London, hung about with scornful women and burdened with an active conscience. 'He's trying to be a good man,' his wife says in a radio interview. It will be interesting to see how he fares.

13 June, 1976

March of the androids

THE *Six Million Dollar Man* (Thames) has acquired a steady girlfriend, called Bionic Woman. Since either of them, in a careless moment, would be capable of pushing over a building with one hand, the question arises of how they manage their love life.

Although a fairly steady follower of Six's adventures, I long ago forgot which bits of him have been replaced with high-performance hardware. The eyes and legs for certain, and at least one arm. It would be indelicate to speculate whether the more intimate sections of his bodily fabric are similarly crammed with transistors and solenoids. The same inhibition applies to discussing some of the attributes of Bionic Woman. But even granting that the two lovers remain organic in those areas, they would still surely be capable of doing each other fearful damage in the spasms of rapture. Six can carve a doorway through a brick wall with his index finger. Imagine what he could do with a single misplaced caress. He could break every circuit in her body. They'd be lying there in a heap of wires and a puddle of hydraulic fluid.

Cultural analysts in the future will no doubt make much of our current preoccupation with bionic man, which in all probability reveals a profound lack of faith in the chances of the standard model to survive and prosper. And by that time the truth might have been established about what is now only a matter of suspicion – that bionic man is already with us, not just in fictional but in factual form. What else is Terry Wogan, for example, but a Six Million Dollar Man with a shamrock in his buttonhole?

As a radio compère Wogan gives a reasonably convincing impersonation of a human being, but for all we know his fluent line of patter might be coming off a cassette. On television, particularly when he hosts *Come Dancing* (BBC1) – the latest series of finals has now, alas, drawn to an end – his eyes are a dead giveaway. They catch the light like quartz, and when the camera goes close you can practically see those little range-finding etched grids on them, just like Six.

Wogan's is a bionic smile if I ever saw one. My guess is that the BBC built him in their own workshops, under licence from General Dynamics. Unfortunately they had to skimp slightly on the brain. Hughes Electronics wouldn't come through with the advanced technology for anything else but cash on the nail, so the Beeb's engineers had to solder together their own version on a restricted budget.

Nevertheless he does very well. Programmed with standard phrases denoting enthusiasm ('Feeling's already running high here at the Lyceum') he maintains an even tone of involved enjoyment while the teams of dancers go through their endlessly repetitive routines. This is where bionic man scores: he can keep a straight, if stiff, face where an ordinary person would either burst out crying or collapse with the giggles.

An increasing number of the dancers themselves look bionic, too — which is perhaps how they manage those sudden manoeuvres in the tango that by rights ought to result in slipped discs and snapped Achilles tendons. In the Grand Final between Scotland and Midland-West, a Scots girl in the cha-cha-cha kicked herself in the head. I thought at the time that this might have been a misguided attempt to score points, but now realise that it must have been a power-surge. And the growing presence of Japanese competitors is easily explained, once you accept the possibility that Sony and Honda might be branching out into a new field.

The Japanese couples, all with names like Micky and Suzy Sokatumi, have been looking better each year. It's because at the end of the European season they get shipped straight back to Japan for re-design. No wonder all those characters in their entourage wear white overalls and carry slide-rules. And that big Datsun van parked outside is full of spare components — swivelling hip-units for the samba, power-assisted right elbows for the military two-step.

This Week (Thames) had an excellent documentary on franchise selling rackets, called 'Get Poor Quick'. Pronto snack-bars, Medi-search energy-replacement drink machines, Happy Hampers fast foods and similar questionable ventures were all revealed to be run by the same overlapping cast of characters, who are permanently in business even though their actual companies fold one after the other. What they are really selling is an idea – the idea of 'a second income that could quickly outstrip your first'. Dejected gullibles who had handed over their life-savings in return for worthless promises were interviewed. More remarkably, some of the men who had made the promises were filmed with a hidden camera. Like all good con-men, they appeared to convince even themselves. The fantasies they were projecting seemed to spring from the all-too-human need to paint glowing pictures. It was the suckers who looked bionic. Perhaps they were still in shock.

Whicker (Yorkshire) was still Down Under, this time interviewing three odd poms who had built a life for themselves in the South Land. There was a jokey bishop, a surfie and a gung-ho brigadier. Despite their claims to individuality, they all had the six million dollar look: the only thing they lacked was aerials. Whicker himself, however, is obviously organic. Nobody would build a machine as eccentric as that. The same goes for Malcolm Muggeridge, currently fronting a drone-in called *Stop to Think* (BBC2). Aided by learned panellists, Muggeridge hopes that we will storp to think about topics sent in by viewers on post-cords. The atmosphere surrounding the panel is more self-congratulatory than electric, except in the sense that a certain tang of ozone hints at the presence of non-organic structures under the epidermis of the guests. But the host was definitely bred rather than built. A Muggeridge machine would have been back to the factory for re-programming long ago.

Horizon (BBC2) says watch out for the sun: it's misbehaving. One of its products, the neutrino – such a *gay* little particle, only showing up as a line of bubbles in shampoo – is not arriving here in sufficient quantities. Hence, presumably, the sinking pound.

20 June, 1976

Onward to Montreal

THE gymnastics and the swimming have finally been got out of the road, the *Olympics* (BBC1 recurring) set-tled down to the task of boring you rigid with the track and field events.

For the Beeb's harassed commentators it was hard to know how to follow that climactic moment at the swimming pool when David Wilkie won a gold medal and Alan Weeks had an orgasm. So loud was the shouting from the com-mentary box that it was sometimes difficult to sort who was screaming what. Hamilton Bland, Alan's new technical assistant, is not very quiet even when he is talking normally. 'But tonight the Union Jack is raised and is being waved very proudly indeed!' 'A proud Scot!' 'And so the big moment has arrived!' 'The Flying Scotsman!' 'We have a certain gold medallist!' All these were among the things yelled, but the loudest bellow of all was unmistakably Alan's: 'David Wilkie is absolutely superb!' And so he was. It was a proud moment for England. Well, Britain. All right, Scotland. What? Oh yes, and the University of Miami.

But when the focus shifted to track and field our patriots found themselves starved of material. Ron Pickering tried to ward off the encroaching void by co-opting new words, of which his favourite was 'absolutely', as in 'We're absolutely short of medals.' And we absolutely were. Nor did the Canadian television people seem to care very much about our plight. Ron was clearly distressed when we weren't even allowed to see Geoff Capes being red-flagged on his last put, the director having cut away to watch a Russian girl getting nowhere in the javelin. And in the 10,000 metres Brendan Foster ('We had such high hopes of Brendan Foster') barely got into shot during the final stages, leaving

Ron to speculate that he might be 'thinking of that plane-load of supporters from Gateshead'.

What Frank Bough constantly referred to as 'Britain's medal-tally' depended absolutely on whether our athletes lived up to our high hopes when it came to the big one. Although the big one is more David Vine's term than Ron's, nevertheless Ron is apt to help himself to it in the heat of the moment, as he did in the women's javelin, where one of the competitors was commended for having managed to 'pull out the big one'. A variation was the longer one, as in 'He's got a longer one out.' And one of the pole-vaulters called forth a burst of eroticism verging on the lyrical. 'Just before he slots it in you'll see him whip it up around his ears ... keeping his left arm absolutely firm ... carrying it parallel to the ground ... '

Even before the Olympics started, David Coleman was already grappling with the problem of how to describe East Germany's Renata Stecher. 'The big girl, Renata Stecher' and 'East Germany's powerful Renata Stecher' were two of the devices he resorted to then. By the time of the Games proper, he was obsessed. 'Stecher really *very* squarely built.' 'Really square. Very, *very* strong.' 'The bulky figure of Renata Stecher.' With regard to Renata, the age of chivalry is dead. The erstwhile attempts to establish that she is really quite feminine off the field have been given up, and nobody now pretends that she wouldn't roll straight over you like a truck.

As in the Winter Olympics, there was heavy use of 'This', 'The man' and 'The man who,' with perms and combs of all three. Thus we heard about 'The man they said couldn't win the big one', 'This the girl we've seen before', 'This the technique to follow', 'This the race', 'The man who's writing a thesis on the psychological effects of world-class sprinting' and 'This the man who didn't want to compete in this'. As a recompense, 'situation' was largely eschewed, except when Ron said that a race was 'getting pretty close to the middle situation', meaning that it was almost half over.

But if 'situation' was on its way out, 'a lot to do' was plainly on its way in. 'Jenkins has a lot to do' was a new way of saying that our man, of whom we had such high hopes, was not going to pull out the big one. A variation was 'an awful lot to do', as in 'and Ovett's got an awful lot to do!', meaning that our man was about to finish an awful long way behind the man who didn't want to compete in this.

Another term in vogue was 'Olympic history', which differs from ordinary history in being rewritten from minute to minute, so that 'the fastest man in Olympic history' can become 'the second fastest man in Olympic history' in just the time it takes someone to pull a longer one out. But all these new locutions paled into insignificance beside the sudden importance of 'ham-string' and 'Achilles tendon'.

With the possible exception of the Queen, everybody at the Olympic Games pulled a ham-string or an Achilles tendon. Sonia Lannaman, of whom we had such high hopes, pulled a ham-string and was unable to compete in her two sprint events. Alan Pascoe failed to recover fully from his pulled ham-string. Maria Neufville fell in her event, having had 'a lot of trouble … with Achilles tendons.' Lucinda Prior-Palmer's horse went lame after a clear round. One Spanish horse went lame from merely looking at the first fence. The logical conclusion was that everybody concerned – man, woman or beast – was trying to do more than nature permits.

To agonise about our medal-tally is absurd. If our medal-tally were larger, there would be real reason for worry, since it would mean that Britain was more concerned with sporting prestige than any free nation of its size ought to be. In the Olympic Games it is neither important to win nor important to have taken part. Sport is just something people who feel like doing it do, up to the point where the effort involved becomes inhuman. Beyond that point, politics takes over. Politically, the Olympic Games are a farce on every level. It is grotesque that in 1976 the BBC commentators should still be sounding like old Pathé Pictorials, desperately cherishing an illusion of British influence which would be fatuous even if it were real.

1 August, 1976